Essential Data Analytics

Quick-Start Guide to Data Literacy for Beginners

Dr. Alex Harper

Table of Contents

Chapter 1: Introduction to Data Literacy

Importance of Data Literacy in Today's World

In a world where every swipe, click, and transaction generates data, the ability to understand and interpret this data has become essential. Data literacy is not just a skill for data scientists or IT professionals; it's a critical competency for nearly everyone. From making informed personal decisions to succeeding in a data-driven job market, data literacy empowers individuals to navigate the complexities of modern life with confidence.

This chapter will explore why data literacy is vital in today's world, shedding light on the role data plays in every industry, its impact on society, and the benefits that individuals and organizations gain from becoming data-literate. By the end of this chapter, you'll understand why data literacy is a foundational skill that can boost your effectiveness and decision-making, setting you up for success throughout this book and beyond.

What is Data Literacy?

Before diving into its importance, let's clarify what data literacy actually means. Data literacy is the ability to read, interpret, understand, and communicate data. A data-literate person can critically analyze data to make informed decisions. They know how to interpret graphs, charts, and tables, and they can recognize patterns, trends, and outliers. Data literacy goes beyond simply understanding numbers; it involves asking the right questions, understanding data sources, and assessing the quality and reliability of data.

Why Data Literacy Matters

1. **Informed Decision-Making** Data literacy enables people to make more informed choices, whether for personal finances, health, career development, or business strategies. For instance, when buying a car, understanding data about fuel efficiency, safety ratings, and resale value can help you make a more informed decision. In the business world, data literacy allows managers and employees to base their decisions on solid evidence rather than guesswork.
2. **Navigating the Information Age** We live in an era defined by the constant flow of information. News, social media posts, and marketing content bombard us daily, often loaded with data or statistics. A data-literate individual can critically evaluate this information, spotting biased or misleading data and differentiating between reputable and unreliable sources. This skill is essential for making sound judgments and staying well-informed.
3. **Increasing Workplace Relevance** Data literacy is increasingly a key asset in the workplace. As businesses strive to be more data-driven, employers are actively seeking employees who can understand and work with data. Regardless of industry—whether in healthcare, finance, education, or marketing—data literacy enhances an employee's ability to analyze trends, measure success, and provide insights that drive organizational success.
4. **Empowerment through Knowledge** Data literacy empowers individuals to harness the potential of data. It's a transformative skill that allows you to take control of the information around you, identifying insights that might otherwise go unnoticed. For example, a basic understanding of data can help you track and improve your fitness, budget, or even identify trends in your productivity.

How Data Shapes Our World

The importance of data literacy becomes even more apparent when considering the influence data has on global decisions, public policy, and the economy. Governments use data to make decisions about public health, education, transportation, and environmental protection. Corporations analyze data to create products, design services, and innovate. Even nonprofits rely on data to allocate resources effectively and measure the impact of their initiatives.

Consider some real-world scenarios:

- **Healthcare**: Data analysis helps doctors make accurate diagnoses, track disease trends, and provide better patient care. In the case of the COVID-19 pandemic, data literacy was crucial for understanding infection rates, hospital capacity, and vaccine efficacy.
- **Environmental Sustainability**: Data literacy is also essential in addressing global issues like climate change. Understanding data on carbon emissions, deforestation, and temperature increases informs policies and behaviors that contribute to sustainable practices.
- **Education**: In education, data is used to personalize learning, improve teaching strategies, and track student progress. Schools increasingly rely on data to understand and address learning gaps, enhancing outcomes for students.

These examples illustrate that data isn't just a corporate or governmental tool—it's at the core of almost every decision that impacts society.

The Benefits of Becoming Data-Literate

Becoming data-literate comes with a range of benefits:

- **Enhanced Personal Decision-Making**: Data literacy empowers you to make well-informed choices, whether it's in your personal or professional life. By understanding data, you can weigh options more objectively, saving time, money, and effort.
- **Improved Critical Thinking**: Data literacy sharpens your critical thinking skills. It encourages you to ask the right questions, consider multiple perspectives, and avoid common cognitive biases. With these skills, you can approach problems methodically and make logical, evidence-based decisions.
- **Increased Job Market Competitiveness**: A data-literate professional is a valuable asset in today's job market. Data skills, even at a foundational level, make you more competitive in nearly every field. You'll be able to back up your opinions with data, impressing employers with your ability to contribute to data-driven projects.
- **Ability to Spot Misinformation**: Data literacy helps you spot "fake news" or misinformation by evaluating data critically. You'll be better equipped to challenge questionable statistics, understand data context, and protect yourself from being swayed by misleading claims.

Common Misconceptions About Data Literacy

1. **"Data Literacy is Only for Data Scientists"** Many people believe that data literacy is only for technical professionals, but that's far from true. While data scientists dive deeply into complex algorithms and machine learning, data literacy is about having the foundational skills needed to work with data at any level.
2. **"You Need to Be Good at Math"** Another misconception is that data literacy requires advanced math skills. While

some familiarity with numbers is helpful, data literacy focuses more on understanding, interpreting, and using data. You don't need to be a math whiz to gain insights from data.

3. **"Data Literacy Requires Expensive Tools"** Many people think that data analysis requires specialized software or costly tools. In reality, you can start developing data literacy using free or accessible tools, like spreadsheets or open-source data visualization software.

The Future of Data Literacy

With the world increasingly turning towards data-driven decision-making, data literacy will only become more important. Schools, businesses, and governments are beginning to prioritize data literacy as an essential skill, just like reading or writing. In the future, data literacy might become a standard part of education, ensuring that everyone has the ability to understand and work with data effectively.

As you continue reading this book, you'll start to see that data literacy is not only an accessible skill but also one that will give you a significant advantage in navigating both personal and professional landscapes.

Real-World Applications and Examples of Data Use

Data isn't just a collection of numbers and facts; it's a powerful tool that drives decisions, shapes strategies, and influences outcomes across various fields. From healthcare to marketing, and education to environmental science, data literacy allows individuals and organizations to make more informed, effective, and strategic choices. In this section, we'll explore some real-world applications of data to illustrate how data literacy transforms the way we live, work, and solve problems.

1. Healthcare: Enhancing Patient Care and Public Health

Healthcare is one of the most data-rich industries, with massive amounts of information generated daily. Medical data, from patient records to lab results, allows doctors and researchers to understand diseases, develop treatments, and improve patient care.

- **Predicting Disease Outbreaks**: During the COVID-19 pandemic, data analysis was essential in predicting hotspots, tracking the virus's spread, and managing healthcare resources. Data from hospitals, governments, and mobile devices helped authorities identify at-risk areas, set travel restrictions, and allocate resources efficiently.
- **Personalized Medicine**: Data has led to significant advancements in personalized medicine, where treatments are tailored based on individual characteristics, like genetics and lifestyle. For instance, analyzing genetic data can help doctors determine which cancer treatments are most likely to work for specific patients, resulting in higher success rates and fewer side effects.
- **Preventive Care and Early Diagnosis**: Data also plays a crucial role in preventive care. Wearable devices, such as fitness trackers and smartwatches, collect data on heart rate, sleep patterns, and physical activity. This information can alert users and healthcare providers to early signs of potential health issues, allowing for timely intervention and improved patient outcomes.

2. Retail and E-commerce: Understanding Consumer Behavior

In retail, data is invaluable for understanding customer preferences, predicting demand, and optimizing inventory. Through data literacy, retailers can turn raw data into insights that drive profits and improve customer satisfaction.

- **Personalized Recommendations**: E-commerce platforms, like Amazon and Netflix, use algorithms to analyze user behavior and recommend products or content that align with individual preferences. This personalization, powered by data on browsing history, past purchases, and demographics, enhances the customer experience and increases sales.
- **Inventory Management and Demand Forecasting**: Data analytics enables retailers to forecast demand accurately, ensuring that popular items are always in stock while avoiding overstocking slower-moving products. For example, by analyzing past sales data and trends, a fashion retailer can predict which clothing items will be in high demand for the upcoming season, allowing them to adjust their inventory accordingly.
- **Pricing Strategies**: Retailers also use data to set competitive prices. Dynamic pricing, for example, adjusts prices based on factors such as time of day, competitor pricing, and demand. Airlines and ride-sharing services, like Uber, frequently use this strategy to maximize profits during peak times while offering discounts during slower periods.

3. Education: Improving Learning Outcomes

In education, data literacy allows educators, students, and administrators to make better decisions about teaching methods, curricula, and resources. Educational institutions increasingly rely on data to improve learning experiences and boost student success rates.

- **Personalized Learning**: Schools and online learning platforms use data to tailor lessons to individual learning styles and abilities. For instance, by tracking a student's progress on assignments, teachers can identify areas where the student struggles and provide targeted support, ensuring a more personalized learning experience.
- **Tracking Student Engagement**: Data analytics can reveal trends in student engagement and participation, helping educators understand what teaching methods work best. For example, if data shows that students engage more with visual materials than with text-based resources, teachers might incorporate more videos and interactive content into their lessons.
- **Predicting Academic Success**: Schools use data to identify students who may be at risk of falling behind, allowing for timely interventions. Early warning systems, based on attendance, grades, and participation data, help schools provide the necessary resources and support to ensure students stay on track.

4. Environmental Science: Tackling Climate Change

Data plays an essential role in addressing environmental challenges, from climate change to biodiversity loss. By analyzing data on natural patterns, scientists and policymakers can make informed decisions to protect the planet.

- **Climate Modeling and Forecasting**: Climate scientists use data from satellite images, weather stations, and historical records to create models that predict climate trends. These

11

models help governments and organizations prepare for climate-related challenges, such as rising sea levels, extreme weather, and changing ecosystems.

- **Conservation Efforts**: Data helps track the populations of endangered species, enabling conservationists to protect habitats and ensure biodiversity. For example, by analyzing data on animal migration patterns, scientists can identify critical areas that need protection, ensuring that species have safe migration routes.
- **Sustainable Resource Management**: Data is also vital for managing natural resources responsibly. By monitoring water usage, deforestation rates, and pollution levels, governments and organizations can develop policies that promote sustainability and minimize environmental impact.

5. Finance: Mitigating Risks and Maximizing Profits

In the finance industry, data literacy is crucial for managing risks, optimizing investments, and understanding market trends. Financial institutions use data to drive their strategies, ensuring both profitability and security.

- **Fraud Detection**: Financial institutions use data to detect unusual patterns and identify potential fraud. Machine learning algorithms analyze transactions in real time, flagging activities that deviate from a customer's typical behavior, such as large international purchases or sudden account withdrawals.
- **Investment Decisions**: Data analysis informs investment decisions, helping investors understand trends and assess the potential risks and rewards of different options. By analyzing market trends, historical performance, and

economic indicators, investors can make data-driven choices to maximize returns.

- **Credit Scoring**: Credit agencies use data to determine individuals' creditworthiness, assessing factors like payment history, outstanding debts, and income. This information helps lenders make informed decisions about whether to approve loan applications, minimizing the risk of defaults.

6. Marketing and Advertising: Reaching the Right Audience

In marketing, data is indispensable for understanding audience demographics, optimizing ad campaigns, and measuring return on investment. Data literacy enables marketers to reach their target audience more effectively and maximize the impact of their efforts.

- **Targeted Advertising**: Marketers use data to segment audiences based on factors like age, location, and interests, allowing them to deliver more relevant ads. For instance, a travel agency may use data to show ads for tropical vacations to users who frequently search for beach destinations.
- **Measuring Campaign Effectiveness**: Data analytics allows marketers to measure the success of campaigns by tracking metrics such as click-through rates, conversion rates, and customer engagement. This information helps them refine their strategies and allocate resources to the most effective channels.
- **Customer Sentiment Analysis**: By analyzing data from social media and customer feedback, companies can gauge public sentiment about their brand or products. This information allows marketers to address concerns, improve products, and build stronger customer relationships.

7. Sports: Improving Performance and Fan Engagement

Data has become a key element in professional sports, where teams, coaches, and players use it to gain a competitive edge and enhance fan engagement.

- **Player Performance Analytics**: Coaches and sports analysts use data to assess player performance, track improvement, and identify areas for growth. For example, in basketball, data on shooting accuracy, speed, and endurance allows coaches to develop training programs tailored to each player's needs.
- **Game Strategy and Tactics**: Data analysis provides insights into team performance, enabling coaches to make strategic adjustments. In soccer, for instance, data on players' positioning and movement patterns can help coaches devise more effective game plans and improve teamwork.
- **Fan Engagement**: Sports teams also use data to improve the fan experience, offering personalized content, promotions, and merchandise. For instance, analyzing data on fan preferences helps teams create engaging experiences, from tailored social media posts to targeted offers.

The Power of Data Literacy in Everyday Life

As these examples demonstrate, data literacy is transforming diverse sectors and impacting people's daily lives. Understanding how data informs these fields can inspire you to see the potential of data in your own life, whether for personal decision-making, career advancement, or contributing to global challenges. As you continue through this book, you'll learn the skills to become more data-literate, empowering you to use data effectively in both professional and personal contexts.

Overview of Data Analytics as a Skill

Data analytics is the process of examining datasets to draw conclusions and make decisions based on evidence rather than intuition or assumptions. In today's world, where data is generated at an astonishing rate, the ability to interpret and analyze data is a powerful and highly sought-after skill. This section will delve into what data analytics involves, the key skills required, and why mastering data analytics is essential for individuals in a variety of roles.

By understanding the scope of data analytics and its applications, you'll gain a foundation for the practical skills you'll learn in the following chapters.

What is Data Analytics?

Data analytics encompasses a range of activities, from data collection and cleaning to statistical analysis and visualization. At its core, data analytics is about transforming raw data into meaningful insights that can guide decision-making. Data analytics is not a single process but rather a collection of skills and methods that work together to achieve specific goals, such as predicting future trends, identifying correlations, or uncovering patterns.

Here's a basic framework of the data analytics process:

1. **Data Collection**: The first step is gathering data from various sources. This could include surveys, databases, logs, or even web-scraped information. Effective data

collection ensures you have reliable data to work with and a solid foundation for further analysis.

2. **Data Cleaning and Preparation**: Raw data is often messy, with duplicates, errors, or missing values. Data cleaning involves processing the data to make it usable, which might include removing irrelevant information, filling in missing values, and standardizing formats.
3. **Exploratory Data Analysis (EDA)**: EDA is the stage where analysts look at the data to uncover initial insights, visualize patterns, and formulate hypotheses. This often involves generating summary statistics and creating simple charts to understand the data's structure.
4. **Data Analysis and Modeling**: This is where analysts apply statistical methods or machine learning algorithms to extract deeper insights from the data. Depending on the goal, this could involve predictive analytics, correlation analysis, or clustering.
5. **Data Visualization**: Presenting data in a visual format—such as graphs, charts, or dashboards—helps make complex information more understandable and actionable for stakeholders.
6. **Reporting and Decision-Making**: Finally, the insights from data analysis are communicated in reports or presentations, guiding decision-makers on the best actions to take based on the data.

By following these steps, data analytics allows professionals to gain meaningful insights and make data-driven decisions that lead to better outcomes.

Key Skills in Data Analytics

Mastering data analytics requires a combination of technical skills, critical thinking, and communication abilities. Here's an overview of some of the key skills involved:

1. **Data Collection and Management Skills**
   - Knowing where and how to gather data is essential for analytics. Skills in SQL (Structured Query Language) or data scraping tools are useful for retrieving data from databases or the web.
   - Data management, which includes organizing and storing data efficiently, is crucial for ensuring that datasets are accessible, reliable, and ready for analysis.

2. **Statistical Analysis and Critical Thinking**
   - Understanding basic statistics is fundamental in data analytics. Skills in measures of central tendency (like mean and median), variability (such as standard deviation), and probability help analysts interpret data accurately.
   - Critical thinking allows analysts to question assumptions, identify biases, and avoid jumping to conclusions. This skill is invaluable for ensuring that insights are accurate and meaningful.

3. **Programming Skills**
   - Familiarity with programming languages like Python or R is highly beneficial for data analytics. These languages offer powerful libraries (such as Pandas for Python) that simplify data manipulation, analysis, and visualization.
   - Programming allows analysts to automate repetitive tasks, handle large datasets, and apply complex algorithms that would be challenging to execute manually.

4. **Data Visualization**
   - Effective data visualization is essential for communicating insights. This skill involves creating graphs, charts, and infographics that make data easy to interpret and highlight key findings.
   - Tools like Tableau, Power BI, or even Excel can be used to create visualizations that tell a story and help stakeholders understand the data's implications.
5. **Domain Knowledge**
   - Knowing the industry or field in which the data is being analyzed is also beneficial. For example, data analytics in healthcare may involve understanding medical terminology and health metrics, while analytics in finance requires knowledge of economic indicators and financial principles.
   - Domain knowledge allows analysts to ask the right questions, understand the context of the data, and provide insights that are relevant and valuable to the organization.

Why Data Analytics is an Essential Skill

1. **Enhanced Decision-Making** Data analytics enables individuals and organizations to make better decisions by providing evidence-based insights. For example, in business, analytics can help determine which products to stock based on past sales trends or which marketing strategies lead to the highest engagement. Data-driven decisions are often more accurate and effective, minimizing risks and maximizing returns.
2. **Problem Solving and Innovation** Data analytics is a powerful tool for problem-solving. By analyzing data,

individuals can identify issues that may not be apparent at first glance. For instance, in manufacturing, data analysis can uncover inefficiencies in production processes, allowing companies to make improvements and reduce costs. Analytics also fosters innovation by revealing new opportunities or potential market segments.

3. **Competitive Advantage** For businesses, data analytics provides a competitive edge by revealing insights that drive strategic initiatives. Companies that leverage data can better understand their customers, predict market trends, and stay ahead of competitors. For individuals, data analytics skills can enhance employability, as many employers seek professionals who can interpret and use data effectively.

4. **Efficiency and Automation** Data analytics also enables automation, making processes more efficient. For instance, retail companies can use data to automate inventory restocking based on sales forecasts, or financial firms can use data analytics to automate fraud detection. These efficiencies save time, reduce manual labor, and allow employees to focus on more strategic tasks.

5. **Adaptability in a Data-Driven World** The ability to work with data makes individuals more adaptable in an increasingly data-driven world. As data becomes more integral to every aspect of business and daily life, individuals with data analytics skills will be better prepared to adapt to new roles, technologies, and challenges. This skill set is not only valuable now but will continue to grow in importance as technology advances.

Examples of Data Analytics in Action

1. **Marketing Campaign Optimization** Data analytics allows marketers to measure the performance of campaigns in real-

time. By analyzing metrics such as click-through rates, engagement, and conversion rates, marketers can adjust their strategies on the fly, allocate budgets more effectively, and target specific demographics with precision.

2. **Customer Segmentation** In retail, data analytics helps businesses understand their customers better. By segmenting customers based on purchase history, demographics, and behavior, companies can create targeted marketing campaigns that cater to specific customer needs, increasing satisfaction and loyalty.

3. **Operational Efficiency** Manufacturing and logistics companies use data analytics to optimize their supply chains. By analyzing data on production times, shipping costs, and inventory levels, these companies can identify bottlenecks, reduce waste, and streamline their operations, ultimately saving costs and improving delivery times.

4. **Risk Management in Finance** Financial institutions rely on data analytics for risk management. By analyzing transaction histories and patterns, banks can identify unusual activity, flag potential fraud, and assess the creditworthiness of loan applicants. Data analytics thus plays a key role in minimizing financial risks.

5. **Public Health Surveillance** Data analytics is essential in public health for tracking and controlling diseases. By analyzing data from hospitals, labs, and even social media, health organizations can monitor outbreaks, identify high-risk areas, and allocate resources to the communities that need them most.

Developing Your Data Analytics Skillset

Learning data analytics is like learning a new language. It takes time, practice, and patience, but it's an investment with immense rewards. This book is designed to guide you through the key components of data analytics, from understanding basic statistics to creating impactful visualizations. Each chapter will build on the concepts introduced here, equipping you with the knowledge to use data confidently and effectively.

Chapter 2: Understanding Basic Data Concepts

Definitions: Data, Information, and Knowledge

At the heart of data literacy lies an understanding of the fundamental concepts of data, information, and knowledge. These three terms are often used interchangeably, but each has a distinct meaning and plays a unique role in the process of gaining insights and making decisions. By differentiating between data, information, and knowledge, we set the stage for more effective data analysis and interpretation.

In this chapter, we'll explore what these terms mean, how they relate to each other, and how they form a hierarchy of understanding—from raw data to actionable insights. By understanding the distinctions, you'll be better prepared to work with data in meaningful ways, ultimately turning it into valuable knowledge.

What is Data?

Data is the raw, unprocessed facts and figures that are collected from various sources. It lacks context and meaning on its own and is often presented as numbers, text, or symbols. Data can be anything from sales figures to temperatures, survey responses, or even website traffic statistics. When we first encounter data, it is typically in its most basic form, without any interpretation or structure.

For example:

- A spreadsheet containing monthly sales figures, but without any analysis or explanation.

- The number of likes a post receives on social media, isolated from other engagement metrics.
- Results from a survey, such as a list of ages or geographic locations of respondents.

Data can be **qualitative** or **quantitative**:

- **Qualitative data** describes qualities or characteristics and is often non-numeric (e.g., colors, types of products, names, or locations).
- **Quantitative data** involves numbers and can be measured, counted, or expressed in numeric form (e.g., number of products sold, temperature, or revenue figures).

Data can also be categorized as **structured** or **unstructured**:

- **Structured data** is organized in a specific format, often in tables or spreadsheets, making it easy to search, organize, and analyze. For instance, a database of customer information with columns for names, emails, and purchase history is structured data.
- **Unstructured data** lacks a predefined format and can include text, images, videos, and audio files. Social media posts, emails, and customer feedback are common examples of unstructured data.

What is Information?

Information is data that has been processed, organized, or structured in a way that adds context and meaning. When data is put into a specific format or analyzed in a way that answers questions or provides context, it becomes information. Information allows us to understand "what happened" and provides the foundation for decision-making.

For example:

- When monthly sales data is summarized to show total sales by product category, it becomes information that can reveal popular and underperforming products.
- A chart displaying the number of website visitors by day provides information on traffic patterns, helping website owners understand peak times.
- Survey results that have been categorized to show the percentage of customers who prefer certain features add insight into customer preferences.

Data vs. Information Example: Let's say you have data on daily temperatures for a city over a month. The raw temperature values are simply data. However, if you calculate the average temperature for each week and then create a report on how temperatures have fluctuated, you've converted that data into information. Now, the temperature trends provide more context, helping us understand weather patterns over that month.

In essence, information is **data interpreted to answer specific questions** and often has a defined purpose. While data is the raw material, information is the processed output that can guide decision-making and further analysis.

What is Knowledge?

Knowledge is the culmination of data and information, combined with insights and expertise. Knowledge involves understanding the relationships and patterns within the information and knowing how to apply this understanding to make informed decisions. In other words, knowledge is information that has been synthesized, contextualized, and internalized to solve problems or predict outcomes.

Knowledge typically involves:

- **Applying insights** gained from information to understand why something happened or to predict what might happen in the future.
- **Leveraging experience** and expertise to interpret information within a broader context, making it more meaningful.
- **Using judgement** to draw conclusions, identify patterns, and make strategic decisions.

For example:

- A manager with knowledge of past sales trends and customer preferences might use current sales information to forecast demand and set inventory levels.
- A healthcare provider uses knowledge derived from patient data and medical research to diagnose and treat patients more effectively.
- A financial analyst with knowledge of market trends uses stock performance data and other economic indicators to make investment recommendations.

Information vs. Knowledge Example: Consider a retailer analyzing customer feedback. The feedback data, when summarized and categorized (information), may show that customers are frequently complaining about delayed deliveries. However, by combining this information with knowledge of the company's shipping process and market demand, the retailer gains knowledge about why delays are happening, allowing them to make informed changes to improve the delivery experience.

In the transition from data to knowledge, context and expertise play a crucial role. While information tells us what happened, knowledge tells us why it happened and what we can do about it. Knowledge enables actionable insights, bridging the gap between understanding data and making impactful decisions.

The Data-Information-Knowledge Hierarchy

To further illustrate the relationship between data, information, and knowledge, let's consider them as steps in a hierarchy:

1. **Data**: Raw, unprocessed facts that lack context. Example: Daily sales figures.
2. **Information**: Data that has been processed, organized, or analyzed to answer specific questions. Example: Monthly sales totals per product category.
3. **Knowledge**: Insights and understanding derived from information, often combined with expertise, to guide decisions. Example: Understanding which product categories are seasonal bestsellers and planning inventory accordingly.

This hierarchy represents the **flow of understanding** in data analytics. Data is the foundation that feeds into information; information, in turn, is refined into knowledge that supports strategic decisions.

Why Understanding This Hierarchy is Important

Each level of the data-information-knowledge hierarchy has its own value and purpose, and understanding these differences is key to data literacy. When you know where a piece of information falls within this hierarchy, you can better understand how to use it effectively.

- **Recognizing Data's Limitations**: Data alone is not enough to make decisions. Without analysis and context, raw data lacks meaning and could lead to misinterpretations if used prematurely. Recognizing this limitation helps ensure that you don't jump to conclusions based on incomplete information.
- **Turning Information into Actionable Insights**: Information, while valuable, still requires interpretation and understanding to guide decisions effectively. By advancing from data to information to knowledge, you ensure that your actions are based on sound, evidence-based insights.
- **Building Decision-Making Confidence**: Knowledge is what ultimately informs confident decision-making. By moving beyond data and information, you gain a comprehensive understanding that allows you to act strategically, not just reactively.

Practical Examples: Turning Data into Knowledge

Let's walk through a practical example to see how data becomes information and then knowledge.

Scenario: A Retail Store's Monthly Sales Analysis

1. **Data**: The store collects daily sales data on each product sold, including the date, product ID, quantity sold, and sales amount.

2. **Information**: The store organizes the data to show total sales per product category each week. This analysis reveals trends, such as which product categories are popular on weekends versus weekdays.
3. **Knowledge**: By combining this information with knowledge of local events and customer demographics, the store manager realizes that certain products sell better when local schools are on break. This knowledge allows the manager to adjust inventory and marketing strategies around school holidays, maximizing sales.

In this example, the raw data (daily sales figures) alone does not reveal much about customer behavior. When structured into weekly sales information, patterns start to emerge. Finally, by interpreting this information within the context of local events and demographics, the manager gains knowledge that can guide business decisions.

Key Takeaways

- **Data**: The raw, unprocessed facts and figures collected from various sources. It is the building block for information but lacks context or interpretation.
- **Information**: Processed data that has been organized or structured to provide context, answer questions, and reveal trends. It helps in understanding what happened.
- **Knowledge**: Information that has been synthesized, contextualized, and combined with expertise to provide deeper understanding and guide decision-making.

Understanding these distinctions is the first step to becoming proficient in data analytics. As we move forward in this book, we'll explore how to work with data, transform it into meaningful information, and leverage it to build actionable knowledge. With this foundation, you'll be well-prepared to harness the power of data effectively in any field or context.

Types of Data: Qualitative vs. Quantitative, Structured vs. Unstructured

Data can take many forms, each with unique characteristics, uses, and analytical methods. Understanding the types of data you encounter—qualitative vs. quantitative and structured vs. unstructured—is essential for determining how to process, analyze, and interpret it effectively. Knowing these distinctions will allow you to choose the right tools and methods for working with different data sets, ultimately helping you gain more accurate insights.

In this section, we'll break down these fundamental types of data, explain the differences, and discuss examples of each. By the end, you'll have a clearer understanding of how to classify data, which is an important first step in any data analysis process.

Qualitative vs. Quantitative Data

Data is often categorized as either qualitative or quantitative based on its nature and how it is measured. Let's explore the characteristics and applications of each type.

1. Qualitative Data

Qualitative data describes qualities, characteristics, or non-numeric attributes. This type of data is often used to understand opinions, motivations, and experiences, providing a more nuanced view of a subject. Qualitative data can be collected through interviews, observations, open-ended surveys, and even images or videos.

Characteristics of qualitative data:

- **Descriptive**: Qualitative data describes qualities or attributes, such as colors, textures, emotions, or preferences.
- **Non-numeric**: It usually consists of words or categories, making it harder to measure in a traditional sense.
- **Subjective**: This type of data is often open to interpretation, as it reflects personal opinions or perceptions.

Examples of Qualitative Data:

- **Customer Feedback**: Textual responses from a survey asking customers about their satisfaction with a product or service.
- **Observational Notes**: Notes taken during a research study observing participants' reactions or behaviors.
- **Social Media Comments**: User comments on social media platforms that provide insight into customer sentiment.

Uses of Qualitative Data: Qualitative data is commonly used in fields like psychology, marketing, and sociology, where understanding the "why" behind behaviors and choices is essential. For example, companies may analyze customer feedback to identify recurring themes in customer complaints, allowing them to improve products or services.

2. Quantitative Data

Quantitative data is numeric data that can be measured and quantified. This type of data answers questions such as "how many," "how much," or "how often." Quantitative data is essential for statistical analysis because it provides concrete, measurable values.

Characteristics of quantitative data:

- **Numeric**: Quantitative data is expressed in numbers, making it easy to analyze using mathematical and statistical methods.
- **Objective**: Since it is measurable, quantitative data is generally more objective and less open to interpretation.
- **Structured**: It often follows a set structure, like values recorded in tables, making it suitable for statistical tests and trend analysis.

Examples of Quantitative Data:

- **Sales Figures**: Monthly revenue figures for a business, including the total number of items sold.
- **Survey Ratings**: Responses from a survey where participants rate their satisfaction on a scale from 1 to 10.
- **Temperature Readings**: Daily temperature measurements recorded over time.

Uses of Quantitative Data: Quantitative data is widely used in scientific research, finance, healthcare, and business. For instance, a company might analyze sales figures to identify trends over time, allowing them to forecast future demand and adjust inventory levels accordingly.

Structured vs. Unstructured Data

In addition to being classified as qualitative or quantitative, data can also be categorized as structured or unstructured based on its organization. Structured data is highly organized and easy to analyze, while unstructured data is more complex and requires additional processing to extract meaningful information.

1. Structured Data

Structured data is organized into a defined format, typically in rows and columns, making it easily searchable and analyzable. This type of data often resides in databases or spreadsheets, where it can be quickly queried and processed using standard tools like SQL or Excel.

Characteristics of structured data:

- **Organized and Easily Accessible**: Structured data is organized in a way that makes it easy to locate, sort, and analyze.
- **Standard Format**: It is typically stored in databases, with clearly defined fields, making it compatible with traditional data analysis tools.
- **Easily Searchable**: Structured data is formatted for easy retrieval using queries, making it well-suited for real-time analysis.

Examples of Structured Data:

- **Customer Database**: A table containing customer names, addresses, purchase history, and contact information.
- **Inventory List**: A spreadsheet with columns for product ID, name, quantity in stock, and price.

- **Transaction Records**: Bank records listing each transaction with details like date, amount, type (debit or credit), and account balance.

Uses of Structured Data: Structured data is commonly used in business and financial analysis because it's easy to sort, filter, and analyze. For example, a retail company might use structured sales data to calculate monthly revenue, analyze purchase patterns, and create sales forecasts.

2. Unstructured Data

Unstructured data lacks a predefined format or organization, making it more challenging to process and analyze. This type of data often includes text, images, videos, and other formats that do not fit neatly into tables. Unstructured data represents a large portion of the data generated today, particularly with the rise of social media and digital content.

Characteristics of unstructured data:

- **Lacks a Standard Structure**: Unstructured data doesn't follow a uniform format, making it difficult to organize and analyze using traditional methods.
- **Complex and Varied Formats**: It can include text, images, audio, video, and more, often requiring specialized tools for analysis.
- **Challenging to Search**: Due to its lack of structure, unstructured data is harder to search and query without advanced tools like natural language processing (NLP) and machine learning.

Examples of Unstructured Data:

- **Social Media Posts**: User comments, tweets, and posts on platforms like Facebook, Twitter, and Instagram.
- **Emails**: The text in emails, which may include both relevant and irrelevant information, attachments, and images.
- **Customer Reviews**: Written reviews on websites like Amazon, Yelp, or TripAdvisor that express customer opinions and experiences.

Uses of Unstructured Data: Although unstructured data is harder to analyze, it contains valuable insights, particularly in understanding customer sentiment, market trends, and user behavior. For instance, companies often use sentiment analysis on social media posts to gauge public opinion about their brand or products. This analysis can reveal trends in customer satisfaction, identify common complaints, and help improve customer service strategies.

Comparing the Types: How They Work Together

Both structured and unstructured data, as well as qualitative and quantitative data, offer unique insights and are often used in combination to provide a comprehensive view. Let's examine some ways these data types complement each other:

1. **Customer Feedback Analysis**
    - **Structured, Quantitative Data**: A survey where customers rate their satisfaction on a scale of 1 to 5 provides structured, quantitative data that can be easily summarized to show the average satisfaction rating.
    - **Unstructured, Qualitative Data**: Open-ended survey responses or social media comments allow

customers to explain their ratings and share specific experiences, providing unstructured, qualitative data.

Combining both types allows companies to quantify customer satisfaction while also understanding the specific reasons behind those ratings, enabling a more holistic approach to customer service improvements.

2. **Market Research**
   o **Structured, Quantitative Data**: Sales figures, demographic information, and purchase histories provide structured, quantitative data that can reveal purchase trends and customer demographics.
   o **Unstructured, Qualitative Data**: Customer reviews, product feedback, and social media posts offer unstructured, qualitative insights into customer preferences and motivations.

By analyzing both types, companies can not only identify popular products and trends but also understand customer sentiments, enabling them to tailor marketing efforts more effectively.

3. **Medical Research**
   o **Structured, Quantitative Data**: Patient records, lab test results, and medication dosage are examples of structured, quantitative data that researchers can use to identify patterns and correlations in health outcomes.
   o **Unstructured, Qualitative Data**: Doctor's notes, patient interviews, and case studies offer

unstructured, qualitative insights into symptoms, treatment experiences, and lifestyle factors.

Together, these data types enable medical professionals to study not only statistical trends but also the personal experiences of patients, leading to more personalized and effective healthcare strategies.

Key Takeaways

- **Qualitative vs. Quantitative**: Qualitative data describes characteristics and is often text-based, while quantitative data involves measurable, numeric values.
- **Structured vs. Unstructured**: Structured data is organized into a specific format, like rows and columns, making it easy to analyze. Unstructured data lacks a predefined format and requires specialized tools to interpret.
- **Combining Data Types**: Many analyses benefit from combining structured and unstructured, qualitative and quantitative data, providing a richer understanding of the subject.

Understanding these types of data equips you with the knowledge to classify data correctly, an essential skill in data literacy. As you progress through this book, you'll learn how to work with each type of data, extracting valuable insights and transforming data into meaningful knowledge.

Introduction to Datasets, Variables, and Data Sources

A crucial part of data literacy is knowing where data comes from, how it's structured, and how to interpret the variables within it. Datasets, variables, and data sources are fundamental components of data analysis, allowing analysts to identify patterns, make comparisons, and draw insights. In this section, we'll break down these concepts, providing definitions, examples, and insights on how they interconnect and contribute to meaningful data analysis.

What is a Dataset?

A **dataset** is a structured collection of data, typically organized in rows and columns. Each dataset contains observations or entries that are recorded on specific variables, providing a comprehensive set of information related to a particular topic. Think of a dataset as a table where each row represents an individual observation (e.g., a customer, product, or transaction), and each column represents a variable describing attributes of those observations.

Characteristics of Datasets

- **Organized Structure**: Datasets are commonly formatted in tables, with each row representing a unique observation and each column representing a variable.
- **Consistency**: Datasets generally maintain a consistent structure, allowing for easy comparison and analysis of observations.
- **Defined Scope**: A dataset often focuses on a specific topic or subject, such as customer demographics, sales data, or scientific measurements.

Types of Datasets

1. **Tabular Datasets**: These are the most common and are arranged in rows and columns, as in a spreadsheet or database table.

2. **Time Series Datasets**: Datasets that track information over time, often used in economics and finance to observe changes in metrics like stock prices or sales volume.
3. **Spatial Datasets**: These include data tied to specific geographic locations, used in fields like geography, urban planning, and environmental science.
4. **Hierarchical Datasets**: These datasets contain nested structures, such as organizational data where each department contains multiple teams, each with several employees.

Examples of Datasets

- **Customer Database**: A dataset containing information on customers, with each row representing a unique customer and columns for attributes like age, location, and purchase history.
- **Financial Transactions**: A dataset that records every transaction made by a business, with rows for each transaction and columns for transaction date, amount, and payment method.
- **Weather Data**: A dataset with daily records of temperature, humidity, and precipitation levels for a specific location, with each row representing a single day.

Understanding Variables

A **variable** is a characteristic or attribute that can be measured or categorized, providing specific information about each observation in a dataset. Variables are the individual columns in a dataset and are essential for analysis, as they allow us to compare, correlate, and assess data in meaningful ways.

Types of Variables

Variables can be classified in different ways based on their properties:

1. **Categorical Variables** (also known as qualitative or nominal variables)
   - Represent categories or groups.
   - Values do not have a numerical significance and cannot be meaningfully added or subtracted.
   - Examples: Gender (Male, Female, Other), Product Category (Electronics, Clothing, Food).
2. **Ordinal Variables**
   - Similar to categorical variables but with an inherent order or ranking.
   - Examples: Education Level (High School, Bachelor's, Master's), Customer Satisfaction (Poor, Fair, Good, Excellent).
3. **Numerical Variables** (also known as quantitative variables)
   - Represent measurable quantities and can be further classified into two types:
     - **Continuous Variables**: Can take any value within a range and are often measured, such as height, weight, or temperature.
     - **Discrete Variables**: Represent countable values, often integers, such as number of products sold, number of employees, or customer age.
4. **Binary Variables**
   - Represent two possible states, typically "yes" or "no," "true" or "false."

      o   Examples: Customer Subscription Status (Subscribed/Not Subscribed), Employee Attendance (Present/Absent).

Examples of Variables in a Dataset

Let's say we have a dataset of customer purchases. Here are some examples of variables we might find:

- **Customer Age**: A numerical variable (discrete) representing the customer's age.
- **Product Type**: A categorical variable indicating the type of product purchased.
- **Purchase Date**: A temporal variable representing the date of purchase, often useful in time series analysis.
- **Purchase Amount**: A numerical variable (continuous) showing the total amount spent on each purchase.

Data Sources: Where Does Data Come From?

Data sources refer to the origin of data. Data can be collected from a wide range of sources, including internal company records, government databases, sensors, surveys, and social media. Understanding the data source is crucial for determining data quality, reliability, and relevance for a specific analysis.

Types of Data Sources

1. **Primary Data Sources**
   - o   Primary data is collected firsthand by the researcher or organization for a specific purpose.
   - o   Examples: Surveys, interviews, observations, and experiments.

- o **Advantages**: Data is specific to the research needs, providing a high level of control and relevance.
- o **Disadvantages**: Collecting primary data can be time-consuming and costly.

2. **Secondary Data Sources**
- o Secondary data is data that was collected by someone else for a different purpose but can be reused for new analysis.
- o Examples: Government reports, industry publications, scientific research papers, and publicly available databases.
- o **Advantages**: Access to a large amount of data without needing to collect it from scratch, saving time and resources.
- o **Disadvantages**: Data may not be tailored to specific research needs and could be outdated or incomplete.

3. **Internal Data Sources**
- o Data generated and stored within an organization, often as a result of day-to-day operations.
- o Examples: Sales records, customer databases, inventory management systems.
- o **Advantages**: Relevant to the organization and often real-time or recent.
- o **Disadvantages**: Limited in scope to the organization's activities and may not provide a comprehensive view.

4. **External Data Sources**
- o Data obtained from outside the organization, providing broader insights into the market or industry.
- o Examples: Market research reports, social media data, government databases.

- o **Advantages**: Can provide context to internal data, helping to benchmark against industry trends.
- o **Disadvantages**: Access may require subscriptions or fees, and external data may not align perfectly with the organization's specific needs.

Examples of Common Data Sources

1. **Publicly Available Databases**
   - o Examples: U.S. Census Bureau, World Bank, World Health Organization.
   - o Uses: Demographic analysis, economic studies, health research.
2. **Social Media Platforms**
   - o Examples: Twitter, Facebook, Instagram.
   - o Uses: Sentiment analysis, brand monitoring, social trend analysis.
3. **Transactional Data**
   - o Examples: Online purchases, in-store transactions, financial transactions.
   - o Uses: Sales analysis, customer behavior studies, inventory management.
4. **Sensor and IoT Data**
   - o Examples: Data from weather sensors, traffic cameras, and fitness trackers.
   - o Uses: Real-time monitoring, predictive maintenance, environmental studies.

Putting It All Together: The Role of Datasets, Variables, and Data Sources in Analysis

Understanding datasets, variables, and data sources is essential for effective data analysis. Here's a summary of how these components work together:

1. **Datasets**: The structured compilation of data relevant to a particular question or study. Datasets are the foundation of data analysis and provide the organized framework within which variables are studied.
2. **Variables**: The specific attributes or characteristics within a dataset that are measured and analyzed. Variables allow us to make comparisons, identify patterns, and extract insights from data.
3. **Data Sources**: The origin of the data, whether collected firsthand or sourced from external repositories. Understanding the source of data is crucial for assessing its reliability, context, and potential limitations.

Practical Example: Analyzing Customer Feedback Data

To illustrate how datasets, variables, and data sources interact, let's consider an example involving customer feedback analysis.

Scenario: A company wants to analyze customer feedback to improve its services.

1. **Dataset**: The company collects data from a survey sent to customers who recently made a purchase. The dataset includes rows representing individual customer responses.
2. **Variables**: The dataset might include the following variables:
    o **Customer Age** (numerical)
    o **Product Purchased** (categorical)
    o **Satisfaction Rating** (ordinal, on a scale of 1 to 5)

      o **Open-ended Feedback** (textual)

3. **Data Source**: The data is collected directly from customers (primary data) using an online survey. This data source provides first-hand insights into customer opinions, ensuring that the feedback is specific to the company's products.

By analyzing this dataset, the company can extract valuable insights. For instance, they may find that satisfaction ratings are lower for a specific product category or identify common themes in the open-ended feedback, such as complaints about delivery time. With this information, the company can make targeted improvements to enhance customer satisfaction.

Key Takeaways

- **Datasets**: Structured collections of data, typically organized in rows and columns, that provide a framework for analysis.
- **Variables**: Attributes or characteristics within a dataset, used to measure and compare observations.
- **Data Sources**: Origins of data that influence its reliability and relevance. Data can come from primary, secondary, internal, or external sources.

Understanding datasets, variables, and data sources is a foundational skill in data analysis, helping analysts organize, interpret, and make informed decisions. In the chapters to follow, we'll dive deeper into working with datasets and manipulating variables to gain meaningful insights.

Chapter 3: Tools of the Trade: Essential Software for Data Analytics

Overview of Commonly Used Tools: Excel, Google Sheets, and Basic SQL

When it comes to data analytics, having the right tools is essential for managing, processing, and analyzing data effectively. While data analytics includes advanced software and specialized programming languages, many powerful analyses can be performed using accessible, commonly used tools like Microsoft Excel, Google Sheets, and SQL. These tools provide a strong foundation, enabling you to perform data manipulation, visualization, and basic statistical analysis, even if you're new to data analytics.

In this chapter, we'll explore how Excel, Google Sheets, and SQL can be used in data analytics, discussing their key features, functionalities, and best practices. By the end, you'll have a clear understanding of how each tool contributes to data analysis, empowering you to choose the best one for your needs.

Microsoft Excel

Microsoft Excel is one of the most widely used tools in data analytics, known for its flexibility, user-friendly interface, and extensive range of functions. Excel is ideal for managing small to medium-sized datasets, performing calculations, and creating visualizations. Excel's versatility makes it a valuable tool for both beginners and experienced analysts.

Key Features of Excel for Data Analytics

1. **Data Organization and Management**
   - Excel allows users to organize data in rows and columns, providing a straightforward structure for managing datasets.
   - Users can sort and filter data to quickly locate specific information or view subsets of data.
2. **Formulas and Functions**
   - Excel includes hundreds of built-in functions for mathematical, statistical, and logical operations. Functions like SUM, AVERAGE, COUNT, and IF make it easy to perform calculations.
   - More advanced functions, such as VLOOKUP, INDEX, and MATCH, allow you to search for specific values and perform complex lookups within the dataset.
3. **Pivot Tables**
   - Pivot tables are one of Excel's most powerful features, enabling users to summarize and aggregate data efficiently.
   - With pivot tables, you can quickly calculate totals, averages, and counts, organize data by categories, and analyze data trends without manually creating complex formulas.
4. **Data Visualization**
   - Excel offers a variety of chart options, including bar charts, line graphs, pie charts, and scatter plots, allowing users to visualize data effectively.
   - Users can customize charts by adding titles, labels, and formatting options, making it easy to communicate insights visually.
5. **Data Analysis ToolPak**
   - Excel's Data Analysis ToolPak is an add-in that provides additional statistical tools, including

regression analysis, histograms, and descriptive statistics.

o These tools are especially helpful for users interested in more advanced analytics, such as hypothesis testing and correlation analysis.

Practical Uses of Excel in Data Analytics

- **Budget Tracking and Financial Analysis**: Excel is widely used for financial planning, budgeting, and forecasting. Analysts can use Excel to track expenses, calculate financial ratios, and project future revenues.
- **Sales and Marketing Analysis**: Marketing teams use Excel to track campaign performance, calculate conversion rates, and analyze customer data to improve strategies.
- **Data Cleaning**: Excel provides various tools for cleaning data, such as removing duplicates, trimming spaces, and converting text to columns. Clean data is crucial for accurate analysis and ensures consistency.

Google Sheets

Google Sheets is a cloud-based spreadsheet tool that offers similar functionality to Excel but with the added advantage of real-time collaboration. It's accessible, easy to use, and provides many of the same formulas and functions found in Excel. Google Sheets is a popular choice for small teams or individuals who need to work on data collaboratively and have access to it from anywhere.

Key Features of Google Sheets for Data Analytics

1. **Real-Time Collaboration**

- o Google Sheets allows multiple users to work on the same spreadsheet simultaneously, making it ideal for team projects and collaborative data analysis.
- o Users can leave comments, suggest edits, and track changes, promoting efficient teamwork.

2. **Formulas and Functions**
   - o Like Excel, Google Sheets offers a wide range of formulas and functions, including basic mathematical operations (SUM, AVERAGE) and more advanced functions (VLOOKUP, FILTER).
   - o Google Sheets also has unique functions, such as IMPORTRANGE (for pulling data from other Google Sheets) and GOOGLEFINANCE (for real-time financial data).

3. **Data Visualization**
   - o Google Sheets includes built-in charting tools, allowing users to create bar graphs, line charts, and pie charts to visualize data.
   - o While the charting options are somewhat limited compared to Excel, Google Sheets is continuously expanding its visualization capabilities.

4. **Add-Ons and Integrations**
   - o Google Sheets offers add-ons that expand its functionality, such as tools for data analysis, automation, and integration with other Google products like Google Forms.
   - o It integrates seamlessly with Google's ecosystem, making it easy to collect data from Google Forms and import it directly into Sheets.

5. **Automatic Backups and Cloud Storage**
   - o As a cloud-based tool, Google Sheets automatically saves changes in real-time, ensuring data is never lost.

      o   Users can access their data from any device with an internet connection, making it highly convenient.

Practical Uses of Google Sheets in Data Analytics

- **Survey Data Collection and Analysis**: Google Sheets integrates with Google Forms, allowing survey responses to be automatically recorded in a spreadsheet for easy analysis.
- **Project Tracking and Collaboration**: Google Sheets is commonly used by project teams to track progress, manage tasks, and collaborate on data analysis.
- **Data Sharing and Accessibility**: Because it's cloud-based, Google Sheets is often preferred when data needs to be accessed by multiple users or shared with external partners.

SQL (Structured Query Language)

SQL, or Structured Query Language, is a programming language designed specifically for managing and querying data in relational databases. While Excel and Google Sheets are effective for smaller datasets, SQL is ideal for working with large datasets and more complex data structures. SQL is widely used by data analysts, data scientists, and database administrators to extract, manipulate, and analyze data stored in databases.

Key Features of SQL for Data Analytics

1. **Data Querying**
   - o   SQL allows users to query data from databases efficiently. The SELECT statement, for example, enables users to retrieve specific columns or rows based on defined criteria.

o Common SQL statements like WHERE, ORDER BY, and GROUP BY allow for filtering, sorting, and grouping data, making it easy to perform focused analysis.

2. **Data Manipulation**
   o SQL includes commands for modifying data within the database. The INSERT, UPDATE, and DELETE commands allow users to add, change, or remove records, maintaining data accuracy.
   o Analysts can use SQL to clean and preprocess data directly within the database, ensuring that it's in the proper format for analysis.

3. **Aggregations and Calculations**
   o SQL includes powerful aggregation functions such as SUM, AVG, COUNT, and MAX/MIN, allowing users to calculate totals, averages, and other summary statistics quickly.
   o By combining these functions with GROUP BY, analysts can calculate aggregated values for different categories within the dataset (e.g., total sales per product category).

4. **Joins for Combining Data**
   o SQL supports various types of joins (INNER JOIN, LEFT JOIN, RIGHT JOIN) that allow users to combine data from multiple tables based on common fields.
   o Joins are essential for relational databases, as they enable analysts to integrate data from different tables, enriching the dataset with additional context.

5. **Data Integrity and Security**
   o SQL databases are designed with built-in mechanisms for data integrity and security. Primary

keys, foreign keys, and constraints ensure that data remains consistent and accurate.

- o Access control features in SQL databases allow administrators to grant or restrict user permissions, maintaining data security.

Practical Uses of SQL in Data Analytics

- **Customer Segmentation**: Analysts use SQL to filter and group customer data by various attributes (e.g., location, age, purchase history) to create targeted marketing campaigns.
- **Financial Analysis**: SQL is used to query and aggregate financial data, allowing analysts to calculate key metrics such as revenue growth, profit margins, and customer lifetime value.
- **Inventory Management**: SQL enables companies to monitor inventory levels, track shipments, and manage stock across multiple locations, ensuring efficient operations.

Comparing the Tools: Choosing the Right One

Each of these tools—Excel, Google Sheets, and SQL—has unique strengths, making them suitable for different tasks within data analytics:

1. **Excel**: Best for small to medium-sized datasets, financial modeling, and data visualization. Excel is ideal for tasks that require flexibility, such as budgeting, project planning, and creating charts.
2. **Google Sheets**: Best for collaborative projects and cloud-based data access. Google Sheets is especially useful for

data collection, team collaboration, and tasks that require accessibility from multiple devices.

3. **SQL**: Best for large datasets, complex queries, and relational database management. SQL is ideal for tasks that involve combining data from multiple tables, performing large-scale aggregations, and managing data in a structured database.

Practical Example: Analyzing Sales Data Across the Tools

Let's consider a scenario where a company wants to analyze monthly sales data across different regions:

1. **Using Excel**: The company's analyst downloads a CSV file of sales data and imports it into Excel. Using pivot tables, they quickly summarize total sales by region and month, creating charts to visualize trends.
2. **Using Google Sheets**: The analyst shares the sales data with their team in Google Sheets, allowing team members from different departments to view, comment, and edit collaboratively. They use conditional formatting to highlight top-performing regions.
3. **Using SQL**: The company's database stores several years of sales data. Using SQL, the analyst queries the database to retrieve monthly sales data by region, calculates average sales per region, and joins tables to add customer demographics. The query results can then be exported for further analysis or reporting.

By understanding these tools and their strengths, analysts can choose the right tool for each task, ensuring efficient and effective analysis.

Key Takeaways

- **Excel**: A versatile tool for data organization, calculations, and visualization, suitable for small to medium-sized datasets.
- **Google Sheets**: A cloud-based spreadsheet with collaboration features, ideal for projects requiring real-time teamwork and accessibility.
- **SQL**: A powerful language for querying and managing large datasets in relational databases, essential for handling complex data structures and large volumes of data.

Each of these tools is foundational for data analysis. As you progress, you'll learn how to leverage their features to extract insights, create visualizations, and make data-driven decisions effectively.

Introduction to Data Visualization Tools: Tableau and Power BI

Data visualization is an essential skill in data analytics, allowing analysts to present complex data in a way that's easy to understand and interpret. While tools like Excel and Google Sheets have basic charting capabilities, specialized data visualization tools like Tableau and Power BI take visual storytelling to a new level. These tools enable users to create dynamic, interactive dashboards that provide insights at a glance, making it easier to communicate data findings to decision-makers.

In this section, we'll explore Tableau and Power BI—two of the most popular data visualization tools in the industry. We'll discuss the unique features of each, how they support data analysis, and why they're invaluable for making data accessible and actionable.

Tableau

Tableau is a data visualization tool known for its intuitive interface, powerful visual capabilities, and ability to handle large datasets. It is widely used by data professionals and organizations to create interactive, visually engaging dashboards that reveal data patterns, trends, and insights.

Key Features of Tableau for Data Visualization

1. **Drag-and-Drop Interface**
   - Tableau's drag-and-drop interface makes it easy to create visualizations without needing extensive technical skills. Users can quickly connect data, choose variables, and build charts by simply dragging fields onto the workspace.
   - This interface allows for fast prototyping of visualizations, making it accessible for beginners while still powerful enough for advanced users.

2. **Wide Range of Visualizations**
   - Tableau supports a variety of visualization types, including bar charts, line charts, scatter plots, heat maps, and geographic maps, enabling users to represent data in diverse ways.
   - The tool allows users to customize visualizations extensively, giving them control over colors, labels, legends, and tooltips, ensuring that the visuals are both informative and visually appealing.

3. **Data Blending and Integration**
   - Tableau can connect to multiple data sources simultaneously, allowing users to blend data from different platforms, such as Excel files, SQL databases, Google Sheets, and online APIs.

o Data blending is particularly useful for combining information from various departments or sources, providing a comprehensive view of the data.

4. **Interactive Dashboards**
   o Tableau enables users to create interactive dashboards that allow viewers to explore data on their own by clicking on filters, hovering over data points, and drilling down into details.
   o Interactive dashboards are particularly valuable for presentations, as they allow stakeholders to explore specific insights relevant to their interests, creating a more engaging data experience.

5. **Geographic Mapping**
   o Tableau has robust geographic mapping capabilities, allowing users to visualize data on maps and analyze patterns based on location. Users can create heat maps, color-coded regions, and pinpoint locations based on geographic variables.
   o This feature is especially useful for industries like retail, logistics, and urban planning, where location-based insights can drive strategic decisions.

6. **Advanced Analytics**
   o Tableau offers advanced analytics features, including trend lines, forecasting, and clustering, which provide deeper insights into the data.
   o With features like calculated fields and statistical modeling, users can go beyond basic visualizations to perform more sophisticated analysis.

Practical Uses of Tableau in Data Analytics

- **Sales Performance Analysis**: Tableau can be used to create dashboards showing sales metrics by region, product category, or sales representative, helping companies track performance and identify high- or low-performing areas.

- **Customer Demographics**: Using geographic mapping and demographic data, analysts can visualize customer distribution, preferences, and purchasing patterns across different regions.
- **Healthcare Data Analysis**: Tableau's interactive dashboards allow healthcare providers to analyze patient data, monitor trends in treatments, and visualize disease prevalence by region, supporting data-driven healthcare decisions.

Power BI

Power BI is a data visualization and business intelligence tool developed by Microsoft. Known for its integration with other Microsoft products, Power BI is popular among organizations that use the Microsoft ecosystem. It provides powerful data visualization capabilities along with tools for data preparation, modeling, and reporting, making it a comprehensive solution for data-driven decision-making.

Key Features of Power BI for Data Visualization

1. **Integration with Microsoft Ecosystem**
   o Power BI integrates seamlessly with other Microsoft applications, including Excel, SQL Server, and Azure, making it ideal for organizations already using these platforms.
   o This integration allows users to import data from various sources within the Microsoft environment easily and link Power BI reports to existing workflows.

2. **Data Modeling and Transformation**
   - Power BI includes tools for transforming and cleaning data before creating visualizations. The Power Query Editor allows users to filter, sort, merge, and modify data directly within Power BI, ensuring that the dataset is ready for analysis.
   - Users can create data models that define relationships between tables, allowing for multi-dimensional analysis and complex reporting.
3. **Customizable Visualizations**
   - Power BI supports a wide array of visualizations, such as line graphs, pie charts, scatter plots, and treemaps. Users can also download custom visualizations from the Power BI marketplace or create their own visuals using the Power BI Developer tool.
   - This flexibility makes Power BI highly customizable, enabling users to tailor visuals to fit their specific analytical needs.
4. **Interactive and Shareable Dashboards**
   - Power BI dashboards are highly interactive, allowing users to explore data by selecting filters, highlighting trends, and drilling down into details.
   - Power BI also offers robust sharing capabilities, allowing users to publish and share dashboards across teams. This feature is valuable for organizations that want to ensure all team members have access to the latest insights.
5. **Natural Language Query (Q&A)**
   - Power BI's Q&A feature allows users to ask questions in natural language (e.g., "What was the total revenue last quarter?"), and Power BI will generate relevant visuals based on the question.

- This feature is particularly helpful for non-technical users, as it makes it easy to generate insights without needing to create complex queries manually.
6. **Data Connectivity**
   - Power BI supports connections to a wide range of data sources, including SQL databases, cloud storage platforms, web-based applications, and flat files. Users can pull in data from services like Google Analytics, Salesforce, and Azure, providing a broad view of an organization's data.
   - Real-time data connectivity also allows users to update dashboards automatically, ensuring they always display the latest data.

Practical Uses of Power BI in Data Analytics

- **Financial Reporting**: Power BI's data modeling and aggregation features allow finance teams to track key financial metrics like revenue, expenses, and profit margins, helping them manage budgets and forecast future financial performance.
- **Human Resources Analytics**: HR teams can use Power BI to visualize employee data, monitor turnover rates, and analyze recruitment metrics, helping them optimize hiring strategies and improve employee retention.
- **Supply Chain Management**: Power BI enables supply chain teams to monitor inventory levels, track supplier performance, and analyze logistics costs, ensuring efficient and cost-effective operations.

Comparing Tableau and Power BI: Choosing the Right Tool

While Tableau and Power BI share many similarities, each tool has its strengths. Here's a comparison to help you decide which tool is best for specific needs:

Feature	Tableau	Power BI
Ease of Use	Intuitive, user-friendly drag-and-drop	User-friendly, especially for Excel users
Integration	Connects with multiple data sources	Strong integration with Microsoft products
Customization	Extensive customization for visuals	Custom visuals available in marketplace
Data Modeling	Limited data transformation capabilities	Robust data modeling and transformation tools
Cost	Generally higher subscription costs	Cost-effective, with a free version available
Best For	Data visualization and interactive dashboards	Comprehensive BI solutions, particularly for Microsoft users

Choosing between Tableau and Power BI depends on factors such as budget, the scale of analysis, data integration requirements, and the tool's compatibility with other software used in the organization.

- **Tableau** is ideal for organizations that prioritize high-quality visualizations, need to connect to a diverse range of data sources, and have larger budgets.
- **Power BI** is an excellent choice for Microsoft-based organizations, as it offers strong integration with Excel and

Azure, is more affordable, and has robust data modeling capabilities.

Practical Example: Analyzing Marketing Data with Tableau and Power BI

Let's explore how a marketing team might use these tools to analyze campaign performance:

1. **Using Tableau**: The marketing team imports data from Google Analytics and social media platforms into Tableau. They create an interactive dashboard showing website traffic, conversion rates, and social media engagement metrics by campaign. With Tableau's geographic maps, they visualize engagement by region, helping them identify areas with the highest response.
2. **Using Power BI**: The team imports the same data into Power BI, linking it with internal sales data stored in SQL Server. They use Power Query to clean and transform the data, ensuring consistency across sources. The team then builds a dashboard that combines engagement metrics with revenue figures, allowing them to measure each campaign's impact on sales. They share the dashboard with the sales team, who can view real-time updates.

Both tools provide valuable insights but in slightly different ways. Tableau focuses on visual appeal and user interaction, while Power BI emphasizes data modeling and integration within the Microsoft ecosystem.

Key Takeaways

- **Tableau**: Known for its powerful visualization capabilities and ease of use, Tableau is ideal for creating visually appealing, interactive dashboards. It's best suited for organizations needing to connect to multiple data sources and prioritize high-quality visuals.
- **Power BI**: A comprehensive BI tool with strong integration within the Microsoft ecosystem, Power BI offers advanced data modeling and transformation features. It's a cost-effective option for organizations using Microsoft products and those needing robust data preparation capabilities.

Both Tableau and Power BI are valuable tools for data analytics, each catering to different needs and preferences. By mastering these tools, you'll be able to create impactful visualizations that make complex data accessible and actionable for decision-makers.

How to Choose the Right Tool for the Task

With so many tools available for data analytics, knowing which one to use for a specific task can be challenging. Each tool—Excel, Google Sheets, SQL, Tableau, and Power BI—has unique strengths, making it more suited to certain types of analysis, data sizes, and reporting needs. This section will provide a guide to selecting the right tool, helping you optimize your workflow, maximize efficiency, and produce the most accurate results.

By understanding the strengths and limitations of each tool, you'll be better equipped to make informed decisions that align with your data analysis goals.

Factors to Consider When Choosing a Tool

Before diving into specific recommendations, it's helpful to consider some key factors that influence tool selection:

1. **Data Size and Complexity**
   - Small datasets with basic calculations and visualizations can often be handled in tools like Excel or Google Sheets.
   - For larger, more complex datasets, SQL is better suited for querying and managing data, while Tableau and Power BI offer strong visualization capabilities for large data.
2. **Data Source and Integration**
   - If your data resides in multiple sources or needs to be integrated from different platforms, a tool with strong data connectivity (like Tableau or Power BI) may be ideal.
   - SQL is also useful for data integration if you're working directly from a relational database.
3. **Type of Analysis**
   - Simple calculations and basic visualizations are easily handled in Excel or Google Sheets.
   - For more advanced analysis, such as statistical modeling, trend analysis, and multi-dimensional analysis, SQL, Tableau, or Power BI may be better options.
4. **Collaboration Needs**
   - For collaborative projects where multiple users need real-time access to data, Google Sheets or Power BI (for Microsoft users) provide the best options.
   - Excel and SQL are more limited in terms of real-time collaboration but can still be effective for smaller teams.
5. **Budget and Accessibility**

- Budget constraints can play a significant role, as some tools require paid licenses (e.g., Tableau, Power BI Pro).
- Google Sheets and Excel offer accessible, budget-friendly options, while SQL, if used with open-source databases, can be highly cost-effective.

6. **Skill Level and Training**
   - Tools like Excel and Google Sheets are generally easier to learn and widely accessible.
   - SQL, Tableau, and Power BI may require some training, especially for users new to data analytics or programming.

Tool Selection by Task

Let's examine some common data analytics tasks and recommend the best tools for each.

1. Data Entry, Cleaning, and Basic Analysis

Recommended Tools: **Excel** and **Google Sheets**

- **Why**: Excel and Google Sheets are both excellent for simple data entry, quick cleaning tasks, and basic calculations. Their interfaces are user-friendly, and they offer functions for sorting, filtering, and basic formatting.
- **Features**:
  - **Excel**: Offers tools like the Data Analysis ToolPak, pivot tables, and conditional formatting for data exploration and cleaning.
  - **Google Sheets**: Provides similar functionalities to Excel, with the added advantage of real-time collaboration.

Use Case Example: A marketing analyst is tasked with cleaning and categorizing customer responses from a recent survey. They use Excel to remove duplicates, sort responses, and apply conditional formatting to categorize answers by sentiment.

Limitations: While Excel and Google Sheets are powerful, they are limited when handling very large datasets or complex data transformation tasks.

2. Querying Large Datasets and Data Preparation

Recommended Tool: SQL

- **Why**: SQL is designed for querying large datasets and extracting data from relational databases. It's highly efficient for data retrieval, filtering, and data manipulation.
- **Features**:
  - SQL can handle complex data extraction with commands like SELECT, JOIN, and GROUP BY, making it ideal for combining tables and creating customized data views.
  - SQL is also effective for data cleaning tasks directly within the database, allowing for efficient data preparation before analysis.

Use Case Example: A sales analyst needs to retrieve sales data from a large database, filtering it by region and product type. Using SQL, they execute a query to extract only the necessary data, reducing the amount of data they need to process and analyze.

Limitations: SQL is less effective for visualization. After querying and preparing data, users may export it to another tool like Tableau or Power BI for visualization.

3. Data Visualization and Dashboard Creation

Recommended Tools: **Tableau** and **Power BI**

- **Why**: Both Tableau and Power BI specialize in data visualization and dashboard creation, enabling users to create dynamic, interactive visuals that support data storytelling and presentation.
- **Features**:
  - **Tableau**: Known for its advanced visualization capabilities and user-friendly drag-and-drop interface, Tableau is ideal for creating high-quality, interactive dashboards.
  - **Power BI**: Power BI offers strong data connectivity and integration with Microsoft products, making it effective for reporting within the Microsoft ecosystem. It's also cost-effective and provides powerful data modeling capabilities.

Use Case Example: An HR team wants to create a dashboard to visualize employee turnover rates, demographics, and department-specific metrics. Using Power BI, they connect to their HR database, transform the data, and build an interactive dashboard accessible to managers across the company.

Limitations: Tableau and Power BI require licenses for full functionality, which may not be cost-effective for small organizations or users with minimal visualization needs.

4. Advanced Data Analysis and Modeling

Recommended Tools: **Excel** (for moderate analysis) and **SQL** (for complex analysis and modeling)

- **Why**: For advanced analysis, such as regression, trend analysis, and clustering, SQL can efficiently handle large datasets and perform complex aggregations. For moderate data analysis, Excel's Data Analysis ToolPak offers tools for regression analysis, ANOVA, and other statistical functions.
- **Features**:
  - **Excel**: The Data Analysis ToolPak includes tools for advanced statistical analysis, while functions like FORECAST and TREND allow for predictive analytics.
  - **SQL**: With advanced SQL functions and stored procedures, SQL can execute large-scale analysis and manipulate data directly within the database.

Use Case Example: A finance team is tasked with performing trend analysis on monthly revenue data. Using SQL, they group the data by year and month, calculate average revenue growth, and identify seasonal trends over several years.

Limitations: SQL is not ideal for data visualization, and Excel's performance may be limited when working with very large datasets. For large-scale visualization of analysis results, Tableau or Power BI may be necessary.

5. Real-Time Data Analysis and Collaboration

Recommended Tool: **Google Sheets** and **Power BI**

- **Why**: Google Sheets is cloud-based, allowing multiple users to collaborate on data analysis in real-time. Power BI's sharing and collaboration features are particularly strong within the Microsoft ecosystem, and it allows for real-time updates if connected to live data sources.

- **Features**:
    - **Google Sheets**: Provides real-time collaboration, making it suitable for teams that need to work on data together from different locations.
    - **Power BI**: Allows users to publish reports and dashboards to the Power BI service, enabling real-time data access and collaboration across teams.

Use Case Example: A product development team is tracking feedback from beta testers in Google Sheets, allowing everyone on the team to access, edit, and comment on the data as responses come in. For high-level summaries, the data can be exported to Power BI, where the team creates a real-time dashboard that updates as new feedback is entered.

Limitations: Google Sheets may struggle with large datasets or advanced analytics, while Power BI's real-time data capabilities may require additional setup and permissions.

Tool Comparison Table

Here's a summary table to help you quickly identify the best tool for common data analytics tasks:

Task	Recommended Tool(s)	Why
Data Entry, Cleaning, and Basic Analysis	Excel, Google Sheets	Simple calculations and data cleaning tasks
Querying Large Datasets	SQL	Efficient data retrieval and filtering for large datasets
Data Visualization and Dashboard Creation	Tableau, Power BI	Advanced visualizations and interactive dashboards
Advanced Data Analysis and Modeling	Excel (moderate), SQL (complex)	Statistical analysis, trend analysis, data modeling
Real-Time Analysis and Collaboration	Google Sheets, Power BI	Real-time collaboration and access to live data

Practical Example: Choosing the Right Tool for a Multi-Stage Analysis

Let's consider a scenario where a retail company wants to analyze customer purchasing behavior across multiple regions:

1. **Data Preparation**: The company has a large database with customer and transaction data. They start by using **SQL** to query and clean the data, filtering for customers who made purchases within the past year.
2. **Exploratory Analysis**: After extracting relevant data, the analyst imports it into **Excel** for exploratory analysis, using pivot tables to understand purchase trends by region and product category.
3. **Visualization**: For presenting the findings, they choose **Tableau** to create an interactive dashboard that shows customer demographics, purchasing behavior, and regional differences. Managers can click on filters to view data by specific regions.
4. **Real-Time Updates**: To keep the dashboard updated, they later shift to **Power BI** and connect it to their SQL

database. This setup allows the team to access real-time customer insights and track purchasing patterns as they evolve.

By using each tool where it performs best, the company gains a comprehensive view of customer behavior, benefiting from SQL's data management, Excel's analytical flexibility, and Tableau and Power BI's visualization strengths.

Key Takeaways

- **Excel** and **Google Sheets** are best for simple data entry, cleaning, and calculations.
- **SQL** is ideal for querying and managing large datasets, especially within relational databases.
- **Tableau** and **Power BI** excel at data visualization, creating dynamic and interactive dashboards that present complex data in an accessible way.
- Choosing the right tool depends on factors like data size, complexity, collaboration needs, and budget.

Selecting the appropriate tool for each stage of analysis ensures efficiency and accuracy, allowing you to leverage each tool's strengths to achieve your data analysis goals effectively.

Chapter 4: Collecting and Cleaning Data

Methods of Data Collection

Data collection is the first step in any data analysis process, as the quality and relevance of the data directly impact the insights that can be gained. Different methods of data collection are used based on the type of analysis, available resources, and specific goals of a project. Understanding these methods helps analysts choose the most effective way to gather accurate and relevant data, setting a solid foundation for subsequent analysis.

In this section, we'll explore the primary methods of data collection, discussing how each works, when to use them, and their advantages and limitations.

1. Surveys

Surveys are one of the most common methods of data collection, particularly for gathering qualitative and quantitative data directly from respondents. Surveys can be conducted online, over the phone, in person, or via mail, making them versatile and widely applicable.

How Surveys Work

- Surveys consist of a series of questions designed to gather information about opinions, behaviors, preferences, or demographic information.
- Questions can be closed-ended (multiple choice, yes/no) or open-ended, depending on the depth of information needed.

- Surveys are typically distributed to a targeted group to ensure that responses represent the desired population or demographic.

Types of Surveys

- **Questionnaires**: Usually self-administered and designed for a wide audience, they can be completed online or in print.
- **Interviews**: One-on-one or group interviews conducted face-to-face, over the phone, or virtually, allowing for more in-depth responses.

Advantages of Surveys

- **Wide Reach**: Surveys can reach large populations quickly, particularly when conducted online.
- **Quantitative and Qualitative Data**: They can gather both numeric data and detailed feedback, providing a balanced view of respondents' opinions or behaviors.
- **Cost-Effective**: Online surveys are relatively inexpensive, especially when compared to in-person interviews or focus groups.

Limitations of Surveys

- **Response Bias**: Respondents may not answer honestly, especially on sensitive topics.
- **Question Design**: Poorly designed questions can lead to misinterpretation or unreliable results.
- **Low Response Rates**: Surveys, particularly online ones, may suffer from low response rates, potentially skewing results.

Example Use Case: A retail company conducts an online survey to understand customer satisfaction with recent purchases, gathering feedback on product quality, service, and delivery speed.

2. Observations

Observation involves collecting data by watching and recording behaviors or events as they occur. This method is particularly valuable in settings where understanding natural behavior is essential, such as in product usability studies, customer behavior analysis, or social research.

How Observations Work

- Observers typically document behaviors, events, or environmental conditions without interfering or interacting with subjects.
- Observations can be structured (using checklists or predefined categories) or unstructured (recording events as they naturally unfold).

Types of Observation

- **Direct Observation**: The observer is present in the environment and watches behaviors firsthand.
- **Participant Observation**: The observer interacts with subjects, often blending into the environment to observe natural behaviors.
- **Remote Observation**: Using video recording or remote monitoring, allowing for later analysis without the observer's physical presence.

Advantages of Observations

- **Real-Time Data**: Captures behaviors and events as they happen, providing immediate, accurate data.
- **Reduced Response Bias**: Observations record natural behavior, reducing the risk of respondents altering their behavior as they might in surveys.
- **Contextual Understanding**: Observation provides insight into the context of behavior, allowing for a deeper understanding of underlying motivations or influences.

Limitations of Observations

- **Time-Consuming**: Observations require a significant amount of time and resources, particularly for long-term studies.
- **Limited Scope**: Observational data is often qualitative, making it difficult to quantify or analyze statistically.
- **Observer Bias**: Observers may unintentionally influence or misinterpret behaviors, especially in unstructured observation.

Example Use Case: A grocery store conducts an observation study to see how customers navigate aisles, revealing insights about product placement and store layout effectiveness.

3. Experiments

Experiments are a method of data collection that involve manipulating one or more variables to observe their effect on another variable. Experiments are often used in scientific, marketing, and psychological research to test hypotheses in a controlled environment.

How Experiments Work

- Experiments consist of a controlled setting where researchers manipulate independent variables to observe their effect on dependent variables.
- They typically involve at least two groups: an experimental group (exposed to the variable) and a control group (not exposed).
- By controlling other factors, researchers can isolate the effect of the independent variable and determine causation.

Types of Experiments

- **Laboratory Experiments**: Conducted in controlled environments where variables can be tightly managed.
- **Field Experiments**: Conducted in real-world settings, where environmental factors are less controlled but results may have higher external validity.

Advantages of Experiments

- **Causal Relationships**: Experiments can establish causation, not just correlation, which is essential for testing specific hypotheses.
- **Control over Variables**: Researchers can isolate variables, reducing the risk of confounding factors.
- **Replicable**: Experiments can be repeated to validate findings, especially in lab settings.

Limitations of Experiments

- **Artificial Environment**: Laboratory experiments may not reflect real-world conditions, limiting external validity.
- **Resource Intensive**: Experiments often require significant resources, including time, personnel, and funding.

- **Ethical Concerns**: Experiments on sensitive topics or vulnerable populations must be designed carefully to avoid ethical issues.

Example Use Case: A skincare brand conducts an experiment to test the effectiveness of a new product. Participants are divided into two groups, with one group using the product and the other using a placebo, allowing researchers to observe differences in skin improvement.

4. Transactional Data

Transactional data refers to data automatically recorded as part of an individual's or organization's daily transactions. This type of data is commonly used in retail, finance, and e-commerce for analyzing trends, customer behaviors, and operational efficiency.

How Transactional Data Works

- Transactional data is automatically generated and recorded whenever a transaction occurs, such as purchases, website clicks, or financial transfers.
- It often includes timestamps, item descriptions, amounts, locations, and customer IDs, providing detailed records for analysis.

Advantages of Transactional Data

- **Automated Collection**: Transactional data is collected automatically, reducing the risk of human error.
- **Large Volumes**: Organizations can collect massive amounts of transactional data, enabling trend analysis and pattern identification.

- **Accurate and Timely**: Recorded in real-time, transactional data provides up-to-date information for immediate analysis.

Limitations of Transactional Data

- **Unstructured**: Transactional data may require significant cleaning and preprocessing to make it suitable for analysis.
- **Privacy Concerns**: Sensitive data may require strict privacy and security measures to protect against unauthorized access.
- **Limited Context**: Transactional data often lacks contextual information, making it difficult to understand the "why" behind behaviors.

Example Use Case: An online retailer analyzes transactional data to understand customer purchase patterns, tracking variables such as purchase frequency, product preferences, and spending habits.

5. Social Media and Web Scraping

Social media and web scraping involve collecting publicly available data from social media platforms, websites, and online forums. This method is increasingly popular for sentiment analysis, trend tracking, and competitive analysis.

How Social Media and Web Scraping Work

- Social media data is gathered from platforms like Twitter, Facebook, and Instagram, where users share opinions, reviews, and preferences.

- Web scraping involves using automated tools to extract data from websites, such as product prices, customer reviews, and blog comments.

Advantages of Social Media and Web Scraping

- **Real-Time Insights**: Social media data offers real-time insights into customer opinions, preferences, and trends.
- **Publicly Accessible**: Web scraping allows analysts to access large volumes of data without needing permissions or direct interaction with respondents.
- **Broad Reach**: Social media and online platforms capture opinions and trends across diverse user demographics.

Limitations of Social Media and Web Scraping

- **Data Quality**: Social media data is often unstructured, requiring significant cleaning and processing.
- **Ethical and Legal Concerns**: Web scraping may violate terms of service for some websites, and privacy concerns must be addressed.
- **Bias**: Social media users may not represent the broader population, leading to skewed insights.

Example Use Case: A company uses social media data to analyze customer sentiment around a recent product launch, identifying common themes in positive and negative feedback.

6. Sensor Data and Internet of Things (IoT)

Sensor data is collected through devices that monitor environmental conditions, machine performance, or human activity. This data collection method is prevalent in manufacturing, healthcare, and environmental science.

How Sensor Data Works

- Sensors detect and measure specific variables, such as temperature, humidity, or movement, and record the data in real time.
- Data is often transmitted through IoT networks, where it can be monitored and analyzed remotely.

Advantages of Sensor Data

- **Real-Time Monitoring**: Sensors provide real-time data, enabling immediate responses to changes or anomalies.
- **Automated Collection**: Data is collected automatically and continuously, reducing human intervention and error.
- **High Volume and Precision**: Sensors generate large datasets with precise measurements, suitable for complex analyses.

Limitations of Sensor Data

- **High Costs**: Installing and maintaining sensors can be expensive.
- **Data Overload**: Sensors produce large volumes of data, requiring advanced storage, processing, and analysis capabilities.
- **Privacy Concerns**: Sensor data in healthcare or personal devices must be managed with strict privacy protections.

Example Use Case: A smart home system collects data on energy usage from various appliances, allowing homeowners to track consumption patterns and reduce energy costs.

Key Takeaways

- **Surveys** are effective for gathering opinions and demographic data directly from respondents.
- **Observations** capture real-time behavior, ideal for studying natural, in-the-moment actions.
- **Experiments** enable researchers to establish causal relationships by controlling variables.
- **Transactional Data** provides accurate, automated records of daily operations.
- **Social Media and Web Scraping** offer real-time insights into public opinion and online trends.
- **Sensor Data** enables continuous monitoring, particularly useful in fields that require precise measurements.

Selecting the right data collection method depends on the type of data needed, the context of the study, and the resources available. Each method has unique advantages and limitations, making it essential to choose the most appropriate method based on your data analysis goals.

Common Data Quality Issues and How to Fix Them

Data quality is critical in data analysis, as inaccurate or inconsistent data can lead to flawed conclusions and misguided decisions. However, raw data often contains errors, inconsistencies, and gaps that must be addressed before analysis. In this section, we'll explore some of the most common data quality issues encountered in analytics, along with practical techniques for identifying and fixing them.

Effective data cleaning is a foundational skill in data analytics and is essential for transforming raw data into a reliable resource for insights.

1. Missing Data

Missing data occurs when values for certain variables are absent in one or more records, which can happen due to human error, data entry issues, or system malfunctions. Missing data can compromise the accuracy of analysis, particularly if the missing values are frequent or concentrated in specific variables.

Types of Missing Data

- **Missing Completely at Random (MCAR)**: The missing values have no pattern and are unrelated to any other variable in the dataset.
- **Missing at Random (MAR)**: The missing values are related to other observed variables but not to the missing values themselves.
- **Missing Not at Random (MNAR)**: The missing values have a specific pattern and are related to the missing variable itself, potentially indicating bias.

Solutions for Missing Data

1. **Deletion**:
   o **Listwise Deletion**: Remove entire rows with missing values. This is appropriate if the missing data is minimal and spread across the dataset.

- Pairwise Deletion: Remove only the specific cells with missing values and analyze the available data. Useful for correlation analysis, as it allows retaining as much data as possible.

2. **Imputation**:
   - **Mean/Median Imputation**: Replace missing values with the mean or median of the variable. This works well for numeric data without extreme outliers.
   - **Mode Imputation**: For categorical data, replace missing values with the mode (most frequent value) of the variable.
   - **Predictive Imputation**: Use a model, such as regression, to predict and fill in missing values based on relationships with other variables.

Example: A dataset has missing values in the "Age" column. You could replace the missing values with the mean age of the dataset or use regression imputation if age correlates with other variables like income or education level.

2. Duplicate Data

Duplicate data refers to records that appear more than once in the dataset, often due to data entry errors or multiple data sources. Duplicates can skew results by overrepresenting certain entries and should be identified and removed during data cleaning.

Solutions for Duplicate Data

1. **Identify Duplicates**:
   - Use built-in functions in tools like Excel or SQL to detect duplicates based on key identifiers, such as names, emails, or unique IDs.

- In SQL, the `DISTINCT` function can be used to remove duplicates in query results.

2. **Remove Duplicates**:
   - **Manual Removal**: For small datasets, manually review and delete duplicate rows.
   - **Automated Removal**: Use data cleaning tools in Excel, Google Sheets, or data management software to identify and remove duplicates quickly.

Example: A customer database has multiple entries for the same customer due to repeat purchases. By filtering for duplicate customer IDs, you can delete duplicate rows, keeping only unique customer entries.

3. Inconsistent Data Formats

Inconsistent data formats occur when data is recorded in different formats across the dataset, making it challenging to analyze. For example, dates might be entered in multiple formats (e.g., "MM/DD/YYYY" vs. "DD-MM-YYYY"), or phone numbers might include varying country codes and delimiters.

Solutions for Inconsistent Data Formats

1. **Standardization**:
   - Convert data to a common format. For example, reformat all dates to "YYYY-MM-DD" or phone numbers to include the country code and consistent separators.
   - Use built-in functions to reformat data. In Excel, the `TEXT` function can convert dates and numbers to consistent formats, while in SQL, date and string

functions like FORMAT or CAST can standardize formats.

2. **Validation Rules**:
   o Set up validation rules to ensure that new data entries follow the correct format. This is especially useful for recurring data collection or automated data entry systems.

Example: A dataset includes dates recorded as both "01/05/2024" and "2024-05-01." By applying a consistent format (e.g., "YYYY-MM-DD"), you ensure that all dates are uniformly represented, enabling accurate time-series analysis.

4. Outliers

Outliers are data points that deviate significantly from the rest of the dataset. They can occur due to measurement errors, data entry mistakes, or natural variability. Outliers can heavily influence statistical analysis, leading to skewed results or inaccurate conclusions.

Solutions for Outliers

1. **Identify Outliers**:
   o Use visualizations, such as box plots or scatter plots, to detect unusual values.
   o Calculate statistical measures like the interquartile range (IQR) or standard deviation. Values that fall outside 1.5 times the IQR or 3 standard deviations from the mean may be considered outliers.
2. **Handle Outliers**:

- o **Removal**: If the outliers result from data entry errors or measurement issues, consider removing them.
- o **Transformation**: Apply log transformations or normalization techniques to reduce the impact of outliers.
- o **Winsorizing**: Cap outliers to a specified percentile, such as the 5th and 95th percentiles, to reduce their influence without removing them entirely.

Example: In a dataset of annual incomes, one entry shows an income of $5,000,000, which is significantly higher than the typical values. After verifying that it's not a data entry error, you might cap it to the 95th percentile to prevent it from skewing the analysis.

5. Inaccurate Data Entry

Inaccurate data entry occurs when values are incorrectly recorded, often due to human error. Common issues include misspelled names, incorrect numerical values, and misplaced decimals. Inaccurate entries can reduce data reliability and lead to misleading results.

Solutions for Inaccurate Data Entry

1. **Data Validation**:
   - o Use validation rules in Excel or Google Sheets to limit values to specific ranges, formats, or lists, reducing the likelihood of incorrect entries.
   - o For numeric data, set logical constraints (e.g., a minimum and maximum range) to prevent impossible values.

2. **Automated Tools**:
    - o Use data cleaning software or programming languages like Python and R to identify anomalies in numeric fields or unusual strings in text fields.
    - o Spell-checkers or natural language processing (NLP) techniques can help correct misspelled text entries.

Example: A survey dataset includes entries for "United States," "USA," and "U.S." as country names. To ensure consistency, you can replace all variations with a single standardized value, such as "USA."

6. Inconsistent Categorical Values

Inconsistent categorical values occur when data in categorical fields (e.g., gender, department, product category) is recorded with slight variations, such as typos or abbreviations. This can lead to redundant categories and unreliable summaries.

Solutions for Inconsistent Categorical Values

1. **Data Standardization**:
    - o Standardize categorical values by choosing a single term for each category. For example, replace all instances of "M" and "Male" with "Male."
    - o Use lookup tables or conditional formatting to quickly identify and replace inconsistent values.
2. **Automated Matching**:
    - o For large datasets, use automated matching algorithms or data-cleaning tools to detect and merge similar categorical values.

Example: In an employee database, the department field includes entries such as "HR," "Human Resources," and "human resources." Standardizing all variations to "HR" ensures consistency, enabling accurate reporting and analysis.

7. Data Redundancy

Data redundancy occurs when the same data is repeated unnecessarily, often due to merging datasets from different sources or duplicate entries. Redundant data can lead to larger file sizes and potential inaccuracies in analysis.

Solutions for Data Redundancy

1. **Database Normalization**:
   o If working within a relational database, normalize the data by dividing it into related tables. This minimizes redundancy while preserving data integrity.
2. **De-Duplication Tools**:
   o Use de-duplication functions in software tools like Excel, Google Sheets, or SQL to remove redundant entries.
   o In SQL, use the `DISTINCT` function or `GROUP BY` clause to filter out repeated data entries.

Example: A CRM system has duplicate customer records due to importing data from multiple sources. By running a de-duplication process, the company removes redundant entries, reducing storage costs and improving data accuracy.

8. Non-Standard Units and Measurement Scales

Data often contains values recorded in different units (e.g., kilograms vs. pounds) or measurement scales (e.g., Celsius vs. Fahrenheit). Non-standard units make it challenging to compare or aggregate data accurately.

Solutions for Non-Standard Units and Measurement Scales

1. **Unit Conversion**:
   o Convert all values to a single standard unit. For instance, convert all weights to kilograms or all temperatures to Celsius.
   o Use formulas in Excel or conversion functions in programming languages like Python to standardize units across the dataset.
2. **Add Metadata for Units**:
   o Clearly label units within the dataset to avoid confusion. For example, include "(kg)" or "(lbs)" in column headers to indicate measurement units.

Example: A dataset records temperatures in both Celsius and Fahrenheit, creating inconsistencies. Converting all temperatures to Celsius provides a uniform basis for analysis, enabling accurate calculations and comparisons.

Key Takeaways

- **Missing Data**: Addressed through deletion or imputation methods, depending on the extent and type of missing values.
- **Duplicate Data**: Detected and removed using automated functions or manual review to prevent overrepresentation.

- **Inconsistent Data Formats**: Standardized to ensure uniformity, especially for dates, phone numbers, and text fields.
- **Outliers**: Identified through statistical measures or visualizations, then handled through removal, transformation, or capping.
- **Inaccurate Data Entry**: Reduced through data validation rules, spell-checking, and automated error detection.
- **Inconsistent Categorical Values**: Standardized to ensure uniformity in categories, reducing redundancies and improving accuracy.
- **Data Redundancy**: Minimized through normalization, de-duplication, or data matching algorithms.
- **Non-Standard Units**: Standardized through unit conversions, ensuring consistency in analysis.

By addressing these common data quality issues, you create a reliable, clean dataset that supports accurate and meaningful analysis, improving the overall integrity of your insights.

Data Cleaning Basics: Removing Duplicates, Handling Missing Values, and Formatting

Data cleaning is an essential step in data analysis, as raw data often contains inconsistencies, errors, and missing values that can compromise the accuracy of insights. Effective data cleaning transforms raw data into a reliable resource, improving its quality and ensuring that subsequent analysis produces valid results. In this section, we'll cover the basics of data cleaning, focusing on three fundamental tasks: removing duplicates, handling missing values, and standardizing data formatting.

1. Removing Duplicates

Duplicate data refers to repeated entries in a dataset, which can lead to overrepresentation and skewed analysis. Duplicates often occur due to data entry errors, merging datasets from different sources, or system glitches. Identifying and removing duplicates is an important step in ensuring data accuracy.

How to Identify Duplicates

1. **Using Excel**: Excel provides a built-in tool to detect duplicates.
   - Select the range of cells, then go to **Data > Remove Duplicates**. You can specify which columns to consider for duplication.
   - Excel will highlight duplicate entries or remove them directly, depending on your preference.
2. **Using Google Sheets**: Google Sheets offers a similar tool to remove duplicates.
   - Select the data range, then go to **Data > Data cleanup > Remove duplicates**. Check the columns you want to use for duplicate detection.
3. **Using SQL**: SQL is effective for identifying duplicates in large datasets.
   - Use the GROUP BY and COUNT functions to find duplicate entries based on specific columns.
   - For example, the query below identifies duplicate records based on the "customer_id" field:

```sql
Copy code
SELECT customer_id, COUNT(*)
FROM customers
GROUP BY customer_id
HAVING COUNT(*) > 1;
```

How to Remove Duplicates

1. **Listwise Removal**: Delete all rows that contain duplicate values. This method is straightforward but may remove useful data if duplicates are present in only one column.
2. **Partial Removal**: If only certain columns contain duplicates, remove duplicates selectively, retaining unique rows based on a key identifier like a customer ID.

Example: In a customer dataset with multiple entries for the same customer ID, you can filter for unique customer IDs, keeping only one record per customer.

2. Handling Missing Values

Missing data is a common issue in raw datasets, resulting from incomplete entries, system errors, or data collection problems. Ignoring missing values can lead to inaccurate results, so it's essential to handle them effectively. The approach to handling missing values depends on the extent of the missing data and its significance to the analysis.

How to Identify Missing Values

1. **Using Excel**: In Excel, you can filter cells to find blanks or use conditional formatting to highlight cells with missing values.
2. **Using Google Sheets**: Apply filters to columns and select the "Blanks" option to locate missing values.
3. **Using SQL**: Use the IS NULL condition to identify rows with missing values in specific columns.
   - For example:

```sql
Copy code
SELECT *
FROM orders
WHERE customer_id IS NULL;
```

Strategies for Handling Missing Values

1. **Deletion**:
   - **Listwise Deletion**: Remove rows with missing values entirely. This is suitable if missing data is minimal and does not significantly affect the dataset.
   - **Pairwise Deletion**: Remove missing values only for specific analyses, retaining as much data as possible. This approach is useful when performing correlation analysis.
2. **Imputation**:
   - **Mean/Median Imputation**: For numeric data, replace missing values with the mean or median of the column. This is effective for data without outliers.
   - **Mode Imputation**: For categorical data, replace missing values with the mode (most common value) in the column.
   - **Predictive Imputation**: Use a regression or machine learning model to estimate and replace missing values based on relationships with other variables.
   - **Forward or Backward Fill**: In time series data, fill missing values with the previous or next valid entry. This approach is useful for datasets where continuity is important.

Example: A sales dataset has missing values in the "quantity_sold" column. You can replace missing values with the mean sales quantity for more accurate reporting, or use predictive imputation if there's a strong correlation with other variables.

3. Standardizing Data Formatting

Inconsistent data formats are common in datasets, especially when data comes from multiple sources or manual entry. Inconsistent formatting complicates analysis, as data may be recorded in various styles or units. Standardizing data ensures uniformity, making it easier to manipulate, analyze, and interpret.

Common Formatting Issues and Solutions

1. **Dates**:
   - **Issue**: Dates may be recorded in multiple formats (e.g., "MM/DD/YYYY," "DD-MM-YYYY").
   - **Solution**: Convert all dates to a single format, such as "YYYY-MM-DD," to ensure consistency. In Excel, you can use the TEXT function to reformat dates, while in SQL, functions like FORMAT or CAST standardize dates.
   - **Example in Excel**:

     ```excel
     Copy code
     =TEXT(A2, "YYYY-MM-DD")
     ```

2. **Text Case Consistency**:
   - **Issue**: Text values, such as city names or product categories, may appear in different cases (e.g., "new york," "New York," "NEW YORK").

92

- o **Solution**: Standardize text to a single case, such as proper case or uppercase. In Excel, you can use the UPPER, LOWER, or PROPER functions to convert text case.
3. **Numerical Formatting**:
   - o **Issue**: Numerical data may include inconsistent units (e.g., currency symbols, commas as thousand separators).
   - o **Solution**: Remove non-numeric characters (e.g., "$") and ensure all numbers are formatted correctly. In Excel, use the VALUE function to convert text to a numeric format.
   - o **Example**: For a column containing values with commas, such as "1,000," use Excel's "Find and Replace" tool to remove commas and convert values to a consistent numeric format.
4. **Phone Numbers and Addresses**:
   - o **Issue**: Contact information often contains variations in format, including parentheses, dashes, and spaces.
   - o **Solution**: Standardize formats by removing extra characters or adding country codes. In Excel, use custom formatting options or the SUBSTITUTE function to clean up phone numbers.
   - o **Example in Excel**:

```excel
Copy code
=SUBSTITUTE(SUBSTITUTE(A2, "-", ""), "(",
"")
```

Automated Formatting Tools

- **Data Validation**: Set up validation rules in Excel or Google Sheets to enforce specific formats during data entry, helping prevent inconsistencies from the start.
- **Conditional Formatting**: Apply conditional formatting to identify cells that do not match the desired format, allowing for quick corrections.

Example: In an employee database, names are inconsistently recorded as "First Last" or "Last, First." Using text functions, you can standardize all names to "First Last" format, ensuring consistency in the dataset.

Practical Example: Cleaning a Customer Dataset

Let's walk through a practical example where a customer service team needs to clean a dataset containing customer information:

1. **Removing Duplicates**: The team uses Excel's "Remove Duplicates" function to eliminate repeated entries based on unique customer IDs. This ensures that each customer appears only once in the dataset, preventing overrepresentation.
2. **Handling Missing Values**: Some customers are missing contact information. The team fills in missing values for "phone number" with "Not Available" (using mode imputation) and uses listwise deletion to remove rows missing critical data, such as "customer ID" or "email."
3. **Standardizing Formatting**:
   - **Date Format**: All date entries are converted to "YYYY-MM-DD" for uniformity.
   - **Text Consistency**: The "City" column is converted to proper case, ensuring entries are consistently

formatted as "New York" instead of "new york" or "NEW YORK."

- o **Phone Numbers**: All phone numbers are formatted with country codes and standardized spacing for easier readability.

After cleaning the data, the customer service team has a reliable, consistent dataset ready for analysis, enabling them to accurately track and evaluate customer interactions.

Key Takeaways

- **Removing Duplicates**: Duplicate entries are identified and removed using functions in Excel, Google Sheets, or SQL to ensure each record is unique.
- **Handling Missing Values**: Missing data is handled through deletion or imputation techniques, with approaches varying based on the type of data and analysis requirements.
- **Standardizing Formatting**: Uniform formats for dates, text, and numerical values are applied to ensure consistency and simplify analysis.

By following these data cleaning basics, you'll improve data quality and accuracy, laying a strong foundation for meaningful analysis. Effective data cleaning minimizes errors, enhances reliability, and ensures your dataset is ready for insightful and impactful analysis.

Chapter 5: Exploring and Analyzing Data

Descriptive Analytics: Measures of Central Tendency and Variability

Descriptive analytics is the process of summarizing and interpreting data to gain insights into its main characteristics. It helps you understand the general patterns and distribution of data, laying the groundwork for more advanced analysis. In this section, we'll focus on two core aspects of descriptive analytics: measures of central tendency and measures of variability.

Measures of central tendency—mean, median, and mode—help describe the "center" of the data, or where most values cluster. Measures of variability—such as range and standard deviation—reveal how spread out the data points are, indicating the extent to which values differ from each other. Together, these measures provide a balanced view of the data, helping you understand both typical values and the overall diversity within the dataset.

Measures of Central Tendency: Mean, Median, and Mode

Measures of central tendency are used to find the central point around which data values are distributed. Each measure of central tendency provides a unique perspective on the "average" or typical value within a dataset, helping you summarize the data in meaningful ways.

1. Mean (Average)

The mean, often referred to as the average, represents the central value of a dataset by taking into account all values. It provides an overall summary by balancing the values on either side of it. The mean is particularly useful when values are evenly distributed, as it gives a straightforward sense of the "center" of the data.

- **When to Use**: The mean is ideal when you want a quick summary of the data and when values are distributed evenly, without extreme outliers.
- **Example**: In a dataset of test scores, calculating the mean gives you an idea of the average performance of the group. If the mean score is 75 out of 100, you know that, on average, the group performed around this level.
- **Limitations**: The mean can be affected by outliers—values that are significantly higher or lower than the rest of the data. If a dataset contains extreme values, they can pull the mean away from the true center, giving a misleading impression of the "average" value.

2. Median

The median is the middle value in a dataset when all values are ordered from lowest to highest. The median gives a sense of the central point in the data, especially when values are not evenly distributed. Since it isn't affected by extreme values, the median is often used when the dataset has outliers or a skewed distribution.

- **When to Use**: The median is ideal for datasets with outliers or skewed distributions, as it gives a more accurate representation of the "typical" value without being influenced by extremes.
- **Example**: If you have data on household incomes in a neighborhood, the median income will give you a better sense of the typical income than the mean, especially if a few very high incomes skew the data.

- **Limitations**: The median may not fully capture the influence of all data points, as it focuses only on the middle position. This can make it less effective for understanding overall trends when there are no extreme values.

3. Mode

The mode is the most frequently occurring value in a dataset. Unlike the mean and median, which focus on central values, the mode shows which value appears most often. It's especially useful for categorical data, where values represent categories rather than numbers.

- **When to Use**: The mode is helpful when you want to understand the most common value in a dataset, particularly for categorical data (such as color preferences or product types).
- **Example**: In a survey where respondents indicate their favorite fruit, the mode will reveal the most popular choice, such as "apple," providing insight into preferences.
- **Limitations**: The mode may not always provide a meaningful summary, especially if the dataset has many unique values with similar frequencies or if there's no repeating value. Additionally, some datasets may have more than one mode, which can make interpretation more complex.

Measures of Variability: Range and Standard Deviation

While measures of central tendency describe the "center" of the data, measures of variability show how spread out the data points are. Variability provides insights into the consistency or diversity of the data, helping you understand the extent of differences among values.

1. Range

The range is the simplest measure of variability, representing the difference between the highest and lowest values in a dataset. It provides a quick overview of the spread, showing the extent to which values vary.

- **When to Use**: The range is helpful when you need a basic understanding of the spread of values, as it gives you the difference between the maximum and minimum points.
- **Example**: If you're looking at daily temperatures over a month, the range will tell you the difference between the hottest and coldest days, giving a sense of temperature variability.
- **Limitations**: The range can be influenced by outliers, as it only considers the highest and lowest values. This may give a misleading impression of variability if the majority of data points are closer to the mean.

2. Standard Deviation

Standard deviation is a more comprehensive measure of variability, showing how much the values in a dataset differ from the mean. A high standard deviation indicates that values are spread out from the mean, while a low standard deviation means they are clustered closely around it. Standard deviation provides a sense of how "typical" values vary from the central point, making it useful for understanding data consistency.

- **When to Use**: Standard deviation is useful when you want a more detailed understanding of how data points differ from the mean. It's especially valuable in comparing datasets with similar means to see if they vary in terms of consistency.
- **Example**: If you're analyzing the test scores of two classes with the same mean score, the class with the lower standard deviation has scores that are more consistent, while the other class has a wider range of scores.
- **Limitations**: Standard deviation assumes data is symmetrically distributed around the mean, so it may not accurately describe variability in highly skewed datasets. It also doesn't convey the exact range of values, focusing instead on typical deviations from the mean.

Practical Examples of Central Tendency and Variability in Action

Let's consider some real-world examples to see how measures of central tendency and variability work together to provide a full picture of data.

1. **Employee Salaries**: Imagine you're analyzing the salaries within a company.
   o **Mean**: The average salary gives a general sense of employee earnings.
   o **Median**: The median salary might be more informative if there are a few executives with very high salaries, which could skew the mean.
   o **Range**: The range reveals the salary gap between the highest and lowest earners, giving insight into pay equity.

- **Standard Deviation**: A low standard deviation would indicate that salaries are relatively uniform across employees, while a high standard deviation suggests a wide variation in earnings.

2. **Product Review Scores**: Consider a dataset of product review scores, rated from 1 to 5 stars.
   - **Mean**: The average score helps summarize overall customer satisfaction.
   - **Mode**: The mode shows the most common score, indicating the typical rating customers give.
   - **Range**: The range tells you the gap between the best and worst ratings, providing insight into the consistency of customer experiences.
   - **Standard Deviation**: A low standard deviation means most customers have similar views, while a high standard deviation indicates mixed reviews.

3. **School Test Scores**: Suppose a teacher wants to understand her class's performance on a recent exam.
   - **Mean**: The average score gives her a sense of overall class performance.
   - **Median**: The median score shows the middle point, useful if some students scored unusually high or low.
   - **Range**: The range highlights the difference between the top and bottom scores, showing the spread of performance.
   - **Standard Deviation**: A low standard deviation indicates that most students performed similarly, while a high standard deviation suggests diverse performance levels.

Summary of Central Tendency and Variability Measures

Measure	Description	Best Used When
Mean	The average of all values, showing overall level	Values are evenly distributed
Median	The middle value, useful for skewed data	Data has outliers or skewed values
Mode	The most frequent value, ideal for categories	Identifying common categories
Range	Difference between highest and lowest values	Quick sense of data spread
Standard Deviation	Typical deviation from the mean, shows consistency	Detailed view of data consistency

Key Takeaways

- **Mean, Median, and Mode**: Each measure of central tendency offers a different way to understand the typical or average value in a dataset, depending on its distribution and presence of outliers.
- **Range and Standard Deviation**: These measures of variability reveal the extent of differences among values, helping you gauge data consistency and spread.

Understanding these measures equips you to explore datasets effectively, highlighting both typical values and overall diversity. With these insights, you'll be ready to dive deeper into your data, armed with a foundational understanding of its core characteristics.

Visualizing Data Insights with Charts and Graphs

Data visualization is a powerful way to communicate insights, patterns, and trends within a dataset. While tables of numbers provide detailed information, charts and graphs translate this information into visuals that are easier to interpret, enabling viewers to quickly grasp key findings. In this section, we'll cover essential chart types, explaining the purpose of each and the types of data they best represent. Whether you're presenting sales trends, customer demographics, or survey results, choosing the right visualization can make your data more compelling and accessible.

Why Visualize Data?

The goal of data visualization is to simplify complex information, making it understandable and impactful. By transforming data into visual formats, you can highlight important insights, illustrate relationships, and support data-driven decisions. Visualizations can help answer questions such as:

- **How has a metric changed over time?** (e.g., sales growth)
- **How do categories compare to one another?** (e.g., product popularity)
- **What's the relationship between two variables?** (e.g., advertising spend vs. sales)
- **How is data distributed?** (e.g., income levels within a population)

Good visualizations make data insights accessible and engaging, providing context at a glance. Let's look at some common chart types and how they help reveal these insights.

1. Line Charts

Line charts are used to display trends over time, making them ideal for tracking changes, such as monthly sales, website traffic, or stock prices. They plot data points on a continuous line, showing whether values have increased, decreased, or remained stable over time.

When to Use Line Charts

- **Trends Over Time**: Use line charts when you want to show how data changes over time, highlighting peaks, valleys, and trends.
- **Comparison of Multiple Series**: Line charts are also effective for comparing trends across multiple groups. For example, you could compare monthly revenue trends across different product lines.

Example

A business tracks monthly sales over the past year, showing a clear upward trend during the holiday season. The line chart highlights these seasonal fluctuations, allowing managers to plan inventory more effectively.

Key Takeaway

Line charts are straightforward and effective for visualizing time-based data, making them essential for trend analysis.

2. Bar Charts

Bar charts represent categorical data with rectangular bars. Each bar's length corresponds to the value of the category it represents, making it easy to compare quantities across categories. Bar charts can be displayed horizontally or vertically, depending on the preference or context.

When to Use Bar Charts

- **Category Comparisons**: Bar charts are ideal for comparing the size of different categories, such as the number of units sold by product type or customer demographics by age group.
- **Ranked Data**: They're useful for ranking data, as it's easy to see which categories have the highest or lowest values.

Example

A marketing team analyzes social media engagement across platforms. By visualizing the data with a bar chart, they can see that Instagram has the highest engagement, followed by Facebook and Twitter, helping them prioritize their social media efforts.

Key Takeaway

Bar charts are versatile and easy to interpret, making them suitable for comparing categories and ranking data.

3. Pie Charts

Pie charts show proportions within a whole, dividing a circle into segments that represent different categories. Each segment's size reflects the proportion of each category, allowing viewers to quickly see the relative size of each part.

When to Use Pie Charts

- **Showing Parts of a Whole**: Pie charts work best for visualizing data that represents parts of a whole, such as budget allocations or market share percentages.

- **Limited Categories**: They are most effective when the dataset has only a few categories; too many categories can make a pie chart hard to read.

Example

A nonprofit organization displays its budget allocation using a pie chart, showing that 50% goes to programs, 30% to outreach, and 20% to administration. The pie chart provides a clear view of how funds are distributed.

Key Takeaway

Pie charts are useful for representing proportions, but they are best suited for small datasets where categories add up to 100%.

4. Histograms

Histograms are used to visualize the distribution of numerical data by grouping data points into bins (or intervals). They look similar to bar charts but show frequency distributions, helping you see where values cluster and where gaps occur.

When to Use Histograms

- **Distribution Analysis**: Use histograms to understand the distribution of data points, such as the frequency of test scores or income levels within a group.
- **Continuous Data**: Histograms are effective for continuous data, where values are not discrete but fall within a range.

Example

An instructor analyzes the distribution of student test scores using a histogram. The chart reveals that most students scored between 70 and 80, while fewer scored above 90 or below 60, helping the instructor understand the range and average of class performance.

Key Takeaway

Histograms provide insight into the distribution of values in a dataset, allowing you to observe trends, clusters, and outliers within a range.

5. Scatter Plots

Scatter plots show the relationship between two variables by plotting data points on a two-dimensional grid. Each point represents one observation, with its position determined by its values on both the horizontal (x-axis) and vertical (y-axis) axes.

When to Use Scatter Plots

- **Identifying Relationships**: Scatter plots are useful for examining relationships or correlations between two variables, such as income and education level.
- **Spotting Patterns or Outliers**: They are effective for identifying patterns, clusters, and outliers, which can suggest potential trends or anomalies.

Example

A company plots advertising spend against sales revenue, using a scatter plot to see if higher advertising spending correlates with higher sales. The points generally follow an upward trend, suggesting a positive relationship between the two variables.

Key Takeaway

Scatter plots are valuable for visualizing relationships between two variables, helping to identify correlations, clusters, and outliers.

6. Box Plots

Box plots (or box-and-whisker plots) summarize data distribution and highlight data spread, showing the range, median, and variability. They are particularly helpful for identifying outliers and understanding the overall distribution of values within a dataset.

When to Use Box Plots

- **Comparing Distributions**: Box plots are ideal for comparing distributions across multiple groups, such as test scores by class.
- **Outlier Detection**: They are effective for identifying outliers, as any values falling outside the "whiskers" of the box plot are considered unusual.

Example

A researcher compares income levels across different regions using a box plot. Each region's income distribution is represented by a box plot, showing that one region has significantly higher variability and a few outliers.

Key Takeaway

Box plots offer a comprehensive view of data distribution, making them suitable for comparing multiple groups and identifying outliers.

7. Heatmaps

Heatmaps display data in a matrix format, with colors representing values. Darker or more intense colors often indicate higher values, making it easy to identify patterns, trends, or concentrations within a grid.

When to Use Heatmaps

- **Showing Intensity or Density**: Heatmaps are useful when you want to illustrate intensity or density, such as customer activity by day and hour.
- **Correlation Matrices**: Heatmaps are also common for showing correlation matrices, where each cell represents the correlation between two variables.

Example

A website analyzes user activity, using a heatmap to display visit frequency by day and time. The heatmap shows peak activity times with darker colors, helping the team identify when users are most active.

Key Takeaway

Heatmaps are effective for visualizing intensity and patterns within a grid, making them ideal for dense data, correlations, and time-based activity.

Choosing the Right Chart: Summary Table

Here's a summary of each chart type and its best uses, to help you select the right chart for your data insights:

Chart Type	Best For	Key Insights
Line Chart	Trends over time	Highlights changes over time
Bar Chart	Comparing categories	Shows category rankings
Pie Chart	Parts of a whole	Illustrates proportions
Histogram	Distribution analysis	Reveals frequency distribution
Scatter Plot	Relationships between two variables	Identifies correlations and patterns
Box Plot	Comparing distributions, outliers	Shows data spread and outliers
Heatmap	Intensity, dense data patterns	Highlights activity or density

Practical Example: Creating a Sales Dashboard

Suppose a sales team wants to create a dashboard to track monthly sales performance, compare product category popularity, and analyze customer purchase patterns. Here's how they could use different charts:

1. **Line Chart**: Tracks total monthly sales over the past year, revealing seasonal trends.
2. **Bar Chart**: Compares sales across product categories, identifying the best and worst-selling items.
3. **Scatter Plot**: Analyzes the relationship between marketing spend and sales revenue, helping determine if higher marketing budgets lead to increased sales.
4. **Pie Chart**: Shows market share by region, allowing the team to visualize regional contributions to total sales.

By combining these charts, the sales team creates a comprehensive dashboard that provides actionable insights, helping them make informed decisions on inventory, marketing, and sales strategies.

Key Takeaways

- **Line Charts** and **Bar Charts** are versatile, widely used tools for tracking trends and comparing categories.
- **Pie Charts** work well for visualizing parts of a whole but are best for datasets with few categories.
- **Histograms** and **Box Plots** provide insights into data distribution, highlighting clusters, outliers, and spread.
- **Scatter Plots** help identify relationships between variables, while **Heatmaps** are useful for visualizing intensity and dense data patterns.

Choosing the right chart type is essential for effectively communicating your insights. By matching your data to the appropriate visualization, you can create clear, compelling representations that make complex data accessible and informative.

Recognizing Patterns, Trends, and Outliers

Data exploration often involves identifying patterns, trends, and outliers—elements that reveal essential characteristics about the data. Recognizing these elements helps analysts uncover insights, predict future outcomes, and make informed decisions. This section covers the fundamentals of detecting patterns, understanding trends, and spotting outliers, each of which offers unique insights into the data's structure and behavior.

Why Recognize Patterns, Trends, and Outliers?

Recognizing patterns, trends, and outliers is critical because they offer different perspectives on the data:

- **Patterns** reveal repeated sequences, behaviors, or structures that can provide insights into underlying relationships.
- **Trends** show the direction of data movement over time, helping predict future outcomes and understand past changes.
- **Outliers** indicate unusual data points that may signify errors, anomalies, or unique insights into rare occurrences.

By understanding these elements, you can create a richer narrative around your data, helping stakeholders make decisions that are both informed and proactive.

Recognizing Patterns

Patterns are recurring sequences or structures within data that can suggest relationships or dependencies among variables. Recognizing patterns is particularly useful for understanding the general behavior of a dataset, detecting seasonality, or discovering associations between variables.

Types of Patterns

1. **Sequential Patterns**: Patterns where data follows a predictable sequence or order.
   - **Example**: An e-commerce website observes that visits peak during specific hours every day, showing a sequential pattern in user behavior.
2. **Cyclical Patterns**: Patterns that repeat over regular intervals, often related to natural cycles or seasonal events.
   - **Example**: Retailers often see higher sales during holiday seasons, indicating a cyclical pattern that repeats annually.

3. **Spatial Patterns**: Patterns that reveal relationships based on location or geographic data.
   - **Example**: Real estate prices in a city may show spatial patterns, with higher prices in certain neighborhoods compared to others.

How to Recognize Patterns

- **Visual Analysis**: Charts and graphs, such as line charts, scatter plots, and heatmaps, make it easier to observe recurring behaviors.
- **Cross-Tabulation**: Creating tables that categorize data can help identify associations and co-occurrences among variables.
- **Clustering**: Clustering algorithms group similar data points, making patterns among groups more visible.

Example: A restaurant notices a pattern of increased bookings every Friday and Saturday, indicating a predictable sequence in customer behavior that helps with staffing and inventory planning.

Why Patterns Matter

Identifying patterns provides insights into predictable behavior, allowing you to anticipate future occurrences. This can be especially useful in sectors like retail, finance, and manufacturing, where understanding customer or market behavior leads to better planning and resource allocation.

Analyzing Trends

Trends represent the general direction of data points over time, showing how values increase, decrease, or remain stable. Trend analysis is valuable for understanding changes, forecasting future outcomes, and tracking the progress of key metrics.

Types of Trends

1. **Upward Trend**: When data points generally increase over time, indicating growth or improvement.
    o **Example**: A company's revenue shows an upward trend over several quarters, signaling business growth.
2. **Downward Trend**: When data points decrease over time, suggesting a decline or negative performance.
    o **Example**: A reduction in product sales over several months might indicate decreased demand or increased competition.
3. **Stable Trend**: When data points fluctuate minimally, suggesting consistency.
    o **Example**: Monthly customer satisfaction scores that remain consistently high show a stable trend in service quality.

How to Recognize Trends

- **Line Charts**: Plotting data over time on a line chart helps reveal upward, downward, or stable trends.
- **Moving Averages**: Calculating moving averages smooths out short-term fluctuations, making long-term trends more visible.
- **Time Series Analysis**: Advanced statistical methods in time series analysis, such as exponential smoothing, can help forecast trends by considering seasonality and randomness.

Example: A business tracks its website traffic, noticing an upward trend that coincides with a new marketing campaign, indicating that the campaign is likely driving more visitors to the site.

Why Trends Matter

Trends help you understand long-term changes and anticipate future movements, which is essential for strategic planning. Identifying trends allows organizations to capitalize on positive changes, address declines, and monitor the effectiveness of ongoing initiatives.

Spotting Outliers

Outliers are data points that deviate significantly from other observations, either much higher or lower than typical values. Outliers can result from errors, natural variation, or unique occurrences. Identifying outliers is crucial because they can skew analysis results, influence averages, and highlight unusual phenomena that may warrant further investigation.

Types of Outliers

1. **Extreme Values**: Outliers that are exceptionally high or low compared to the rest of the data.
   - **Example**: In a dataset of exam scores, most students score between 60 and 80, but one student scores 100, making it an extreme outlier.
2. **Errors or Data Entry Mistakes**: Outliers caused by incorrect data entry, such as an extra zero added to a number.

o **Example**: An inventory dataset mistakenly records 1,000 units instead of 100, creating a misleadingly high outlier.
3. **Natural Variations**: Outliers that result from genuine but rare events.
   o **Example**: An unusually high sales spike on Black Friday is a natural outlier driven by the holiday season.

How to Spot Outliers

- **Box Plots**: Box plots display the data spread and highlight outliers, making them ideal for identifying unusual values.
- **Scatter Plots**: Scatter plots can reveal outliers that deviate significantly from the main data cluster.
- **Standard Deviation**: If a value is far from the mean and outside the normal range, it is likely an outlier. Standard deviation is a common measure used to determine what counts as a "normal" distance from the mean.

Example: An HR team notices that one employee's annual leave days are significantly higher than the rest of the team. This outlier prompts further investigation, revealing an error in leave recording.

Why Outliers Matter

Outliers can provide meaningful insights or distort analysis, depending on their cause. Identifying outliers helps you decide whether to investigate or exclude them from analysis, ensuring accuracy in trends and averages.

Practical Approaches for Recognizing Patterns, Trends, and Outliers

Let's go through some practical examples of how you might recognize patterns, trends, and outliers in real-world datasets.

1. **Sales Data**: A company tracks monthly sales data across product lines.
   - o **Pattern**: Sales tend to increase every November and December, indicating a seasonal pattern around the holiday season.
   - o **Trend**: Over the past two years, the company sees a gradual upward trend in annual sales, suggesting business growth.
   - o **Outliers**: One month has unusually high sales due to a major promotional event, which stands out as an outlier from regular sales figures.
2. **Website Analytics**: A marketing team monitors weekly website traffic to assess the effectiveness of a new ad campaign.
   - o **Pattern**: Traffic spikes every Friday, suggesting a pattern in user behavior.
   - o **Trend**: There's a steady upward trend in overall traffic, indicating that the campaign is successfully attracting more visitors.
   - o **Outliers**: One week shows an unexpected drop in traffic due to a technical issue, which is easily identified as an outlier.
3. **Customer Feedback Scores**: A company tracks customer feedback scores to monitor service quality.
   - o **Pattern**: Higher scores are consistently reported during certain times of the year, such as the holiday season.
   - o **Trend**: The average customer satisfaction score has gradually improved over time, showing a positive trend.

- o **Outliers**: A few exceptionally low scores suggest isolated incidents of customer dissatisfaction, prompting further investigation.

Tools for Identifying Patterns, Trends, and Outliers

1. **Excel and Google Sheets**:
   - o Use line charts, scatter plots, and conditional formatting to highlight patterns and trends.
   - o Box plots and conditional formatting can help flag outliers visually.
2. **Tableau and Power BI**:
   - o Create interactive dashboards that reveal patterns and trends across different categories and time periods.
   - o Use filters and sorting options to isolate outliers and observe their impact on overall data.
3. **SQL**:
   - o SQL queries can help identify outliers by filtering values that are above or below specific thresholds.
   - o SQL's aggregation functions can reveal patterns, such as peak times for transactions or high-frequency behaviors.
4. **Python and R**:
   - o Python's libraries like Pandas and Seaborn, and R's ggplot2, provide tools for plotting trends, detecting patterns, and spotting outliers.
   - o Statistical libraries help automate calculations for measures like standard deviation to detect potential outliers.

Key Takeaways

- **Patterns**: Repeated sequences or behaviors within data that reveal consistent associations, making it easier to anticipate future occurrences.
- **Trends**: General directions of data change over time, showing upward, downward, or stable movement, essential for forecasting.
- **Outliers**: Unusual data points that differ significantly from others, often signaling errors, anomalies, or rare events.

Recognizing patterns, trends, and outliers allows analysts to gain a deep understanding of their data, providing context, predicting future behavior, and identifying areas that require further investigation. By developing these skills, you'll be able to draw richer insights and support data-driven decision-making in a wide range of scenarios.

Chapter 6: Introduction to Data Visualization

Importance of Data Visualization in Storytelling

Data visualization is a crucial tool for transforming raw data into visuals that are accessible, engaging, and informative. In today's data-driven world, information is abundant but often complex. Data visualization enables us to present this information in ways that are easy to understand, allowing viewers to quickly grasp insights and make informed decisions. Effective data visualization is more than just graphs and charts—it is a storytelling technique that gives data meaning, creating a narrative that resonates with audiences and drives action.

In this chapter, we'll explore why data visualization is so important in storytelling, how it enhances communication, and the ways it makes data more compelling, relatable, and impactful.

Why Data Visualization Matters in Storytelling

The human brain processes visual information far more effectively than text or numbers alone. Visualization transforms complex datasets into visuals that are easier to interpret and understand, bridging the gap between data and insight. By visualizing data, we create a form of storytelling that can communicate trends, patterns, and relationships in a way that resonates emotionally and intellectually with the audience. In business, research, and public communication, the ability to tell stories with data can lead to better decision-making, increase audience engagement, and make an impact.

Key benefits of data visualization in storytelling include:

1. **Enhanced Comprehension**: Visuals help audiences understand data faster and with less cognitive load than text or tables.
2. **Emotional Engagement**: Well-designed visuals evoke emotional responses, helping viewers connect with the message on a personal level.
3. **Improved Retention**: People remember visual information more effectively, which makes visual storytelling memorable and persuasive.
4. **Increased Accessibility**: Visuals make complex data accessible to a broader audience, regardless of technical background.

Let's dive deeper into how data visualization brings storytelling to life.

Creating a Narrative with Data Visualization

Data storytelling combines data, visuals, and narrative elements to communicate insights. While raw data is often overwhelming and abstract, data storytelling helps contextualize information, transforming facts and figures into a coherent message. Effective data visualization provides the backbone for this narrative, helping to structure the story in a way that flows logically and keeps the audience engaged.

Steps to Building a Data Story

1. **Identify the Central Message**: The first step is identifying the main message or insight you want to convey. Rather than overwhelming your audience with numbers, focus on the one key point that you want them to remember.

2. **Organize Data to Support the Story**: Structure your data to reveal patterns, trends, or comparisons that emphasize your main point. The way data is organized and presented directly affects how easily the story unfolds for the audience.
3. **Select Appropriate Visuals**: Different types of data and messages require different visual formats. For example, line charts are ideal for trends, bar charts for comparisons, and pie charts for showing proportions. Choosing the right type of chart or graph is essential to effectively telling the story.
4. **Add Context and Narrative**: Providing context helps the audience understand why the data matters. Adding a narrative element, such as annotations or captions, guides viewers through the story, emphasizing important points and explaining complex information.
5. **Highlight Key Takeaways**: A successful data story should leave the audience with clear takeaways. Use visual cues, like color and font size, to emphasize critical points, ensuring the message is both memorable and actionable.

Example

Imagine you're analyzing customer satisfaction survey results over the past year. You might start by showing a line chart that illustrates the trend in satisfaction scores. Adding annotations about specific events—like a new product launch or a change in customer service policies—helps to connect the data with real-world actions. This context transforms a simple trend line into a story about how company initiatives impact customer satisfaction.

How Visualization Enhances Audience Engagement

Data visualization engages audiences by transforming abstract numbers into tangible, relatable stories. Here's how visualization helps enhance audience engagement:

1. **Immediate Impact**: Visuals capture attention instantly, making it easier for audiences to focus on the story. A well-designed visualization can convey the essence of the message at a glance, allowing audiences to grasp complex information quickly.
2. **Simplification of Complex Data**: Visualizations distill complex datasets into clear, understandable insights, reducing the cognitive load on the audience. This simplification allows viewers to focus on the message without being overwhelmed by details.
3. **Emotional Resonance**: Colors, shapes, and design elements can evoke emotions, which helps to create a deeper connection with the audience. For example, a red color in a chart showing declining sales may trigger a sense of urgency, while a green line indicating upward trends can evoke optimism.
4. **Interactivity and Exploration**: Interactive visualizations, such as those in Tableau or Power BI, allow users to explore the data for themselves. By interacting with filters or drilling down into details, users can personalize their experience, making the data story more relevant and engaging.

Example

Consider a company presenting its annual performance to stakeholders. A static chart showing annual revenue can quickly summarize overall growth, but adding interactive filters for different regions or product lines allows stakeholders to explore specific areas of interest, making the presentation more engaging and informative.

Types of Visualizations that Enhance Storytelling

Choosing the right type of visualization is essential for effective storytelling. Different visualizations are suited to different types of insights, so selecting the most appropriate format helps to communicate your message clearly. Here are some common types of visualizations used in storytelling:

1. **Line Charts**: Ideal for showing trends over time, such as growth in monthly sales or changes in market share.
2. **Bar Charts**: Effective for comparing categories, like sales by product or customer satisfaction by region.
3. **Scatter Plots**: Useful for showing relationships between variables, such as advertising spend versus sales revenue.
4. **Heatmaps**: Great for illustrating intensity or density, such as peak website traffic times.
5. **Pie Charts**: Used for showing proportions within a whole, such as market share or budget allocation.

Each type of visualization has unique strengths, so choosing the right one for your data and message enhances the story you're trying to tell.

Example of Choosing the Right Visualization

If you're telling the story of a successful product launch, a line chart showing sales over time might illustrate the initial boost in revenue. To add depth, a bar chart comparing sales by region can show where the launch was most successful, giving stakeholders a clearer picture of the campaign's impact.

Building Credibility and Trust with Visualization

Data storytelling is not only about engaging the audience but also about building credibility. Visualizations that are clear, accurate, and honest help establish trust with the audience, demonstrating transparency and integrity in reporting.

Key Practices for Building Trust

1. **Avoid Misleading Visuals**: Ensure that charts and graphs accurately represent the data. For example, avoid truncating axes or using overly complex visuals that could confuse or mislead the audience.
2. **Use Consistent Scales**: Consistency in scales across multiple charts allows for accurate comparison, making the story more cohesive and credible.
3. **Provide Context**: Including contextual information, such as timeframes, data sources, or explanations for unusual data points, helps the audience understand the full story and trust the findings.
4. **Be Transparent about Limitations**: If the data has limitations, such as sample size or data collection constraints, openly communicate these limitations to ensure transparency.

Example

A government agency reporting on unemployment rates can use clear, consistent visuals with full context about how data was collected. Including information on the sample size, collection method, and limitations (like seasonal adjustments) helps the public trust the accuracy of the report.

The Role of Visual Storytelling in Decision-Making

Data visualization aids decision-making by providing stakeholders with actionable insights. When data is presented clearly, decision-makers can quickly interpret key metrics, assess performance, and evaluate options. Visual storytelling turns abstract metrics into specific narratives that guide strategy and action.

How Visualization Supports Decisions

- **Clarity of Key Insights**: Well-crafted visuals highlight critical insights, enabling stakeholders to make informed decisions based on clear evidence.
- **Rapid Comparisons**: Visualizations like bar charts and scatter plots allow decision-makers to compare options quickly, facilitating faster, more accurate decisions.
- **Reinforcement of Recommendations**: Visual storytelling supports recommendations by showing the underlying data, making it easier for decision-makers to understand and accept the suggested actions.

Example

A marketing manager presents data on campaign performance using bar charts and line graphs. The visuals reveal which channels performed best, supporting the recommendation to allocate more budget to high-performing channels. The clarity of the visual story gives stakeholders confidence in the recommendation, facilitating data-driven decisions.

The Future of Data Visualization in Storytelling

As technology advances, data visualization continues to evolve, incorporating new tools and techniques that enhance storytelling. From interactive dashboards to augmented reality and virtual reality visualizations, the future of data visualization promises even more engaging, immersive, and insightful ways to communicate data stories.

Emerging Trends in Data Visualization

1. **Real-Time Data Visualization**: Increasingly, businesses rely on real-time data to make agile decisions. Interactive dashboards with live data updates allow stakeholders to track metrics in real time, enhancing responsiveness.
2. **Augmented and Virtual Reality (AR/VR)**: These technologies enable immersive data experiences, allowing users to interact with data in three-dimensional spaces. AR and VR hold promise for industries like architecture, healthcare, and education.
3. **Data Storytelling with AI**: AI-powered data visualization tools can automatically generate narratives, charts, and insights from raw data, making it easier for analysts to build compelling stories without extensive design skills.
4. **Personalized Visualizations**: As more data becomes available, visualizations can be personalized to show relevant insights to different audience segments, making data stories more relevant and actionable.

Key Takeaways

- **Data Visualization as a Storytelling Tool**: Visuals transform complex data into narratives that audiences can understand, connect with, and act on.

- **Engagement and Accessibility**: Visuals simplify data interpretation, increasing audience engagement and making insights accessible to a wider audience.
- **Trust and Credibility**: Clear, honest visualizations build trust with audiences, establishing data storytelling as a credible source of information.
- **Enhanced Decision-Making**: Data visualization supports decision-making by clarifying options, highlighting key insights, and reinforcing recommendations.

The ability to tell stories with data is an invaluable skill in today's information-rich world. Effective data visualization not only makes data more understandable but also empowers audiences to draw meaningful conclusions, make informed decisions, and drive positive change.

Types of Charts and When to Use Each

Data visualization transforms raw data into accessible, engaging visuals that communicate key insights. Choosing the right type of chart is essential for conveying your message effectively. Different charts are suited to different kinds of data and storytelling goals, so understanding their strengths and limitations will help you make the best choice. In this section, we'll review common chart types—bar charts, pie charts, line charts, and more—exploring when and why to use each.

1. Bar Charts

Bar charts use rectangular bars to represent data, with the length of each bar corresponding to the value of the category it represents. Bar charts are versatile, making it easy to compare values across categories.

When to Use Bar Charts

- **Category Comparison**: Bar charts are ideal for comparing values across discrete categories, such as sales by product type, customer satisfaction by region, or survey responses.
- **Ranking Data**: They are effective for ranking data, as it's easy to see which categories have the highest or lowest values.
- **Horizontal or Vertical**: Use vertical bars (column charts) for limited categories and horizontal bars when there are many categories or when labels need more space.

Example

A retail company uses a bar chart to compare monthly sales for different product lines. The chart quickly shows which product lines are performing best, allowing managers to make inventory decisions accordingly.

Variations

- **Stacked Bar Chart**: Useful for showing subtotals within categories, allowing you to see contributions of different sub-categories within each bar.
- **Grouped Bar Chart**: Effective for comparing multiple sub-categories across main categories, such as product sales by month for each region.

Key Takeaway

Bar charts are straightforward and effective for comparing values across categories, making them one of the most commonly used chart types in data analysis.

2. Pie Charts

Pie charts display data as slices of a circle, with each slice representing a category's proportion within a whole. They are often used to show percentages and relative sizes.

When to Use Pie Charts

- **Showing Parts of a Whole**: Pie charts work well for visualizing proportions and illustrating how each category contributes to a total.
- **Limited Categories**: They are most effective when the dataset has only a few categories (ideally less than six), as too many categories make the chart difficult to read.
- **Quick Overview**: Pie charts are best for simple visuals where exact values are not as important as the general distribution.

Example

A nonprofit organization uses a pie chart to show its budget distribution, with segments for programs, outreach, and administrative costs. The pie chart makes it easy for donors to see where their contributions go.

Key Takeaway

Pie charts are useful for illustrating proportions within a whole, but they are best suited for small datasets where categories add up to 100%.

3. Line Charts

Line charts use points connected by lines to display changes over time, making them ideal for tracking trends and patterns in time-series data.

When to Use Line Charts

- **Trends Over Time**: Line charts are ideal for showing data trends across time periods, such as monthly revenue, daily temperatures, or annual growth rates.
- **Multiple Series Comparison**: They are effective for comparing trends across multiple groups. For example, you could compare sales trends for different products over the same time period.
- **Highlighting Change**: Line charts make it easy to see when values increase, decrease, or remain stable, making them useful for tracking progress.

Example

A finance team uses a line chart to track monthly expenses over the past year. The chart shows a gradual upward trend, helping the team spot patterns and adjust budgets.

Key Takeaway

Line charts are essential for visualizing trends and changes over time, making them popular in financial, sales, and performance tracking.

4. Scatter Plots

Scatter plots display individual data points plotted on a two-dimensional grid, with one variable on each axis. This chart type is used to show relationships or correlations between variables.

When to Use Scatter Plots

- **Exploring Relationships**: Scatter plots are useful for examining relationships between two variables, such as age and income, or advertising spend and sales revenue.
- **Spotting Patterns or Clusters**: Scatter plots can help identify patterns, clusters, and outliers within the data, providing insights into potential trends or anomalies.
- **Large Datasets**: Scatter plots are particularly useful for large datasets with numerous data points, as they reveal density and spread.

Example

A company uses a scatter plot to examine the relationship between customer satisfaction scores and loyalty program participation. The scatter plot shows a positive correlation, suggesting that customers in the loyalty program are generally more satisfied.

Key Takeaway

Scatter plots are ideal for showing correlations and relationships between two variables, as well as spotting patterns and outliers.

5. Histograms

Histograms look similar to bar charts but are used to show the distribution of a continuous variable by grouping data points into intervals or "bins." They're commonly used to understand the shape of the data distribution.

When to Use Histograms

- **Distribution Analysis**: Histograms are ideal for understanding the distribution of values, such as age ranges, income levels, or exam scores.
- **Identifying Skewness**: Histograms reveal whether data is skewed to one side (left or right), which can inform data interpretation.
- **Spotting Clusters and Gaps**: They help identify clusters or gaps in data, showing where values are concentrated and where they are sparse.

Example

An instructor uses a histogram to analyze student test scores, revealing that most students scored between 70 and 85. This insight helps the instructor assess overall class performance and identify students who may need extra help.

Key Takeaway

Histograms are valuable for visualizing data distributions, making them useful for identifying patterns, skewness, and clusters in continuous data.

6. Box Plots

Box plots (or box-and-whisker plots) display the distribution and spread of data by dividing values into quartiles. They show the median, range, and variability, making them useful for comparing distributions across different categories.

When to Use Box Plots

- **Comparing Distributions**: Box plots are ideal for comparing distributions across multiple groups, such as test scores across different classrooms or income levels by region.
- **Identifying Outliers**: Box plots highlight outliers, as any points outside the "whiskers" are considered unusual values.
- **Analyzing Spread and Symmetry**: They provide a quick summary of data spread and whether data is symmetrical or skewed.

Example

A healthcare analyst uses box plots to compare patient recovery times across different hospitals. The box plots reveal variations in recovery times, showing which hospitals have shorter recovery periods.

Key Takeaway

Box plots provide a comprehensive view of data spread, making them ideal for comparing distributions, spotting outliers, and understanding data variability.

7. Heatmaps

Heatmaps display data in a matrix format with colors representing values. Darker or more intense colors often indicate higher values, making it easy to identify patterns or clusters within the data.

When to Use Heatmaps

- **Showing Intensity or Density**: Heatmaps are useful for visualizing intensity or density, such as frequency of website visits by hour and day.
- **Correlation Matrices**: Heatmaps are commonly used to show correlation matrices, where each cell represents the correlation between two variables.
- **Large Data Grids**: They are effective for showing large datasets, where each cell's color represents a different value.

Example

A website analyzes user activity, using a heatmap to display visit frequency by day and hour. The heatmap shows peak activity times with darker colors, helping the team identify when users are most active.

Key Takeaway

Heatmaps are effective for visualizing density and intensity within a grid format, making them ideal for time-based data, correlation matrices, and high-density datasets.

8. Area Charts

Area charts are similar to line charts but fill the space below the line with color, emphasizing the magnitude of the trend. They are useful for showing cumulative data or comparing multiple trends over time.

When to Use Area Charts

- **Cumulative Totals**: Use area charts to show cumulative totals over time, such as total sales or revenue.
- **Comparing Multiple Trends**: Area charts are effective for showing multiple data series, with each area representing a different category.
- **Highlighting Proportions Over Time**: They help show how different parts contribute to a total over time, especially when categories stack on each other.

Example

A company uses an area chart to illustrate revenue from various product lines over the past year. The chart highlights how each product line contributes to the overall revenue, with clear distinctions between categories.

Key Takeaway

Area charts are ideal for illustrating cumulative totals and comparing multiple series, especially when showing contributions over time.

Choosing the Right Chart: Summary Table

Here's a summary of each chart type and its best uses, to help you select the right chart for your data insights:

Chart Type	Best For	Key Insights
Bar Chart	Comparing categories	Shows category rankings and differences
Pie Chart	Parts of a whole	Illustrates proportions
Line Chart	Trends over time	Highlights changes over time
Scatter Plot	Relationships between two variables	Identifies correlations and patterns
Histogram	Distribution analysis	Reveals frequency distribution
Box Plot	Comparing distributions, outliers	Shows data spread and outliers
Heatmap	Intensity, dense data patterns	Highlights activity or density
Area Chart	Cumulative totals over time	Shows contribution trends

Practical Example: Creating a Dashboard with Multiple Chart Types

Let's say a company wants to create a dashboard to monitor monthly sales performance, compare product line popularity, and analyze customer behavior. Here's how they might use different charts:

1. **Line Chart**: Tracks monthly sales, showing the overall trend in revenue.
2. **Bar Chart**: Compares sales across product categories, helping to identify top-performing products.
3. **Scatter Plot**: Shows the relationship between marketing spend and sales, helping assess the impact of advertising.
4. **Heatmap**: Displays customer activity by time and day, highlighting peak shopping hours.

By combining these charts, the company creates a comprehensive dashboard that provides a clear, multi-dimensional view of business performance.

Key Takeaways

- **Choosing the Right Chart**: Selecting the correct chart type enhances understanding and effectively communicates insights.
- **Bar Charts and Pie Charts**: Ideal for comparing categories and showing proportions, respectively.
- **Line Charts and Scatter Plots**: Best for trends and relationships between variables.
- **Histograms and Box Plots**: Useful for distribution and variability analysis.
- **Heatmaps and Area Charts**: Effective for visualizing intensity, density, and cumulative totals over time.

Understanding the purpose and strengths of each chart type helps you create visuals that tell a clear, compelling story. By mastering these fundamentals, you can select the best visual for your data, ensuring it resonates with your audience and supports informed decision-making.

Tips for Creating Effective Visuals

Creating effective visuals is key to successful data communication. A well-designed visualization can make complex data easy to understand, highlight key insights, and support decision-making. However, not all visuals achieve these goals—some may confuse or mislead if not designed thoughtfully. In this section, we'll explore essential tips for creating effective data visuals, covering design principles, color choices, layout, and more to ensure your visuals communicate insights clearly and impactfully.

1. Define the Purpose of the Visualization

Before starting any visualization, clarify its purpose. Ask yourself:

- **What insight or message do I want to communicate?**
- **Who is my audience, and what's important to them?**
- **What action do I want viewers to take based on this information?**

Having a clear purpose will guide your design choices, ensuring that each element contributes to the overall message.

Example

If you're creating a visualization for a sales team, your purpose might be to highlight quarterly revenue growth. In this case, you'd focus on a line chart showing trends over time rather than a detailed breakdown of individual sales, which could distract from the main message.

2. Choose the Right Chart Type

Selecting the appropriate chart type is crucial for accurately conveying your data. Each chart type has unique strengths:

- **Bar charts** are ideal for comparing categories.
- **Line charts** work well for showing trends over time.
- **Pie charts** illustrate proportions within a whole.
- **Scatter plots** highlight relationships between variables.

Consider what you're trying to show—comparisons, trends, parts of a whole, or relationships—and choose a chart type that best suits the message.

Example

To show the market share of different product lines, a pie chart would clearly illustrate each line's contribution to total sales. For monthly sales trends, a line chart would be more effective.

3. Simplify and Remove Clutter

When it comes to data visualization, less is often more. Cluttered visuals can overwhelm the audience and obscure the message. Focus on essential information by removing unnecessary elements like gridlines, excessive labels, and decorative graphics that don't add value.

Tips for Simplifying Visuals

- **Limit Color Use**: Use only a few colors to avoid visual noise. Reserve bright colors to highlight key data points.
- **Reduce Labels**: Label only essential elements and use concise titles and annotations.
- **Avoid Excessive Data**: Focus on the most relevant data points, and avoid overcrowding the chart with too much information.

Example

A bar chart comparing sales performance across regions can become cluttered if each bar is labeled with exact values. Simplifying the chart by labeling only the top-performing regions and using a clean title can make the chart easier to interpret.

4. Use Color Purposefully

Color can make visuals engaging, highlight important data, and convey information quickly. However, using color effectively requires careful consideration to avoid confusion or misinterpretation.

Best Practices for Using Color

- **Highlight Key Points**: Use a bold or contrasting color to draw attention to specific data points or categories.
- **Use Consistent Color Schemes**: Choose a color scheme that aligns with your brand or the context of your data. Avoid using too many colors, as this can create visual clutter.
- **Consider Color Blindness**: Use color palettes that are accessible to all viewers. Avoid relying solely on color to convey information—use patterns, labels, or icons to reinforce key points.

Example

In a line chart showing revenue over time, use a neutral color for the baseline trend and a bold color to highlight a period of significant growth. This approach draws attention to the specific period while maintaining a clear overall view.

5. Add Clear Labels and Titles

Effective labels and titles guide the viewer through the visualization, helping them understand the data quickly. Each element—titles, labels, legends, and annotations—should be clear, concise, and placed strategically to enhance readability.

Best Practices for Labels and Titles

- **Use Descriptive Titles**: A good title tells the viewer what the chart represents. Instead of a vague title like "Quarterly Sales," a more descriptive title like "Quarterly Sales Growth by Region" provides context.
- **Label Key Data Points**: If certain data points are particularly important, label them directly on the chart to ensure they stand out.
- **Use Legends Wisely**: Place legends close to the chart and keep them simple. If possible, label data directly to avoid relying on legends, which can make the viewer work harder to understand the chart.

Example

A scatter plot showing advertising spend vs. sales could benefit from a title like "Correlation Between Advertising Spend and Sales Revenue." Adding direct labels to outliers or notable points will also help viewers focus on the most important parts of the data.

6. Use Consistent Scales and Axes

Inconsistent scales and axes can lead to misinterpretation and bias. To ensure clarity, use scales that accurately represent your data and avoid unnecessary manipulation of axis ranges.

Tips for Consistent Scales

- **Start at Zero**: Where possible, start your axis at zero to prevent visual distortion. This is especially important for bar charts, as truncating the axis can exaggerate differences.
- **Use Even Intervals**: Consistent intervals on both axes make comparisons straightforward and prevent misleading impressions.

- **Avoid Overcrowding the Axis**: Keep axis labels readable, using abbreviations or fewer tick marks if necessary.

Example

In a line chart tracking monthly revenue, starting the y-axis at zero will provide a realistic view of growth. If the axis starts at a higher value, the growth could appear more dramatic than it actually is, potentially misleading the viewer.

7. Highlight Key Insights

To emphasize the most critical information, highlight key insights in your visual. This helps guide viewers' attention to the points that matter most, ensuring they leave with a clear understanding of the main takeaways.

Techniques for Highlighting Insights

- **Use Annotations**: Adding text boxes or arrows to highlight significant events, such as peaks, dips, or anomalies, directs the viewer's focus.
- **Adjust Color and Opacity**: Use a distinct color or make other elements more transparent to highlight specific data points.
- **Focus on Key Data Points**: In some cases, you can grey out less relevant data to emphasize the most important insights.

Example

A line chart showing monthly website traffic may have a notable spike during a marketing campaign. By adding a label indicating

"Campaign Launch" on that data point, you emphasize the correlation between the marketing effort and traffic increase.

8. Provide Context with Annotations

Annotations are brief notes added to visuals to provide context, explain anomalies, or highlight trends. They help viewers interpret data by connecting it to real-world events, making the visualization more informative.

When to Use Annotations

- **Explain Anomalies**: Use annotations to clarify outliers or unusual data points, such as a sudden drop in sales due to an external event.
- **Highlight Trends and Changes**: Add notes that explain significant trends, such as the introduction of a new product or a seasonal effect.
- **Add Insights**: Annotations can also be used to add commentary, helping viewers understand why certain data points are important.

Example

In a bar chart comparing quarterly revenue, a note like "Seasonal Increase" next to a peak in Q4 helps viewers understand that this spike is part of an annual pattern, not a permanent increase.

9. Maintain a Balanced Layout

A well-organized layout enhances readability and flow. Balanced visuals avoid overwhelming viewers, presenting information in a logical order that guides them through the data story.

Best Practices for Layout

- **Group Related Information**: Place similar elements together. For example, if you're displaying sales by region, put all regional data visuals in one area.
- **Use White Space**: White space improves readability, giving viewers a break between elements and helping each part of the visual stand out.
- **Establish a Visual Hierarchy**: Prioritize the most important data and place it in a prominent location. Secondary information should be smaller or placed around the main insights.

Example

In a dashboard showing monthly sales, arrange the main revenue chart in the top center. Place secondary charts, such as sales by product or region, around it, creating a clear focal point while still presenting additional context.

10. Test Your Visuals with Others

Finally, testing your visuals with colleagues or stakeholders can help identify potential improvements. Feedback allows you to ensure that your message is clear, relevant, and engaging.

Tips for Testing

- **Gather Feedback from Non-Experts**: Ask someone unfamiliar with the data to interpret the visual. If they struggle, consider simplifying the design or adding more context.

- **Check for Misinterpretations**: Ensure that viewers interpret key points correctly and that there's no ambiguity in your message.
- **Refine Based on Input**: Use feedback to refine color schemes, labels, and layout, improving clarity and effectiveness.

Example

Before presenting a new product sales report, a marketing team shows the visualization to a few team members. Their feedback leads to improvements in label placement and color choice, making the final presentation more polished and effective.

Summary of Tips for Creating Effective Visuals

Tip	Key Insight
Define the Purpose	Focus on the main message
Choose the Right Chart	Match the chart type to the data
Simplify and Remove Clutter	Focus on essential elements
Use Color Purposefully	Highlight important data points with color
Add Clear Labels and Titles	Guide viewers with descriptive labels
Use Consistent Scales	Ensure accurate data representation
Highlight Key Insights	Emphasize the most important points
Provide Context with Annotations	Add notes to clarify data trends and anomalies
Maintain a Balanced Layout	Organize visuals for readability
Test with Others	Get feedback to refine visuals

Key Takeaways

Creating effective visuals is both a science and an art, requiring attention to design principles, clarity, and purpose. By following these tips, you can ensure that your data visuals are clear, engaging, and impactful. Thoughtful visual design enables audiences to understand key insights quickly, supporting informed decisions and meaningful discussions.

Effective data visualization is not just about presenting numbers but about crafting a visual narrative that resonates with audiences and encourages action. With these strategies, you'll be well-equipped to create visuals that communicate your data's story in the most effective way.

Chapter 7: Basics of Data Interpretation and Decision-Making

Understanding the Story Behind the Numbers

Data by itself is just a collection of numbers; the true value of data lies in its interpretation. Data interpretation involves analyzing data in a way that reveals patterns, trends, and relationships that drive understanding and decision-making. By understanding the story behind the numbers, analysts and decision-makers can transform raw data into meaningful insights that tell a story about past events, current conditions, and potential future outcomes.

In this chapter, we'll explore the basics of data interpretation, focusing on techniques for uncovering insights, making informed decisions, and drawing actionable conclusions from data.

Why Data Interpretation Matters

Effective data interpretation is essential because it turns complex information into clear, actionable insights. Raw numbers rarely provide meaning on their own, but interpretation provides context, connects the data to real-world scenarios, and uncovers the narrative hidden in the numbers.

Benefits of Effective Data Interpretation

1. **Informed Decision-Making**: Interpretation provides insights that support data-driven decisions, helping organizations act based on evidence rather than intuition.
2. **Pattern and Trend Recognition**: By interpreting data, we can identify recurring patterns and long-term trends that provide insight into ongoing dynamics.

3. **Risk Management**: Interpreting data helps identify risks and opportunities early, allowing decision-makers to mitigate potential issues before they escalate.
4. **Clear Communication**: Interpretation allows data to be communicated in ways that are accessible and relatable, supporting collaboration and alignment across teams.

Understanding the story behind the numbers brings clarity, which is crucial for effective action and strategy development.

Key Steps in Data Interpretation

Data interpretation is both an art and a science. It involves reviewing the data, identifying relationships, and translating these relationships into a story that answers questions and guides decisions.

Step 1: Define the Goal and Ask the Right Questions

Before diving into data interpretation, it's important to clarify the goal. Understanding what you're looking to achieve or understand will shape how you approach the data and what insights you seek to uncover.

- **What business question am I trying to answer?**
- **What decision will be made based on this data?**
- **What information does my audience need to make this decision?**

These questions help focus your analysis, ensuring you're interpreting the data in ways that are relevant and meaningful.

Example

Suppose you're examining customer satisfaction scores to improve service. Defining the goal as "identifying factors that impact customer satisfaction" helps narrow your focus to specific data points—such as response times or issue resolution rates—that directly relate to the goal.

Step 2: Organize and Clean the Data

Interpretation becomes challenging if data is messy or disorganized. Cleaning and organizing data ensures accuracy and clarity, enabling a clear view of patterns and relationships.

- **Remove Duplicates and Outliers**: Identify and address any duplicate records or outliers that could distort insights.
- **Check for Missing Data**: Handle missing values through imputation or by acknowledging gaps in data.
- **Standardize Formats**: Ensure consistency in units, categories, and date formats to make comparisons valid.

Example

In analyzing monthly sales data, missing entries or incorrect product categories can misrepresent the overall trend. Cleaning and organizing data helps ensure accurate interpretation, reducing the risk of drawing incorrect conclusions.

Step 3: Look for Patterns and Trends

Patterns and trends often tell the clearest stories. Trends show changes over time, while patterns reveal recurring behaviors. Identifying these elements can provide insight into underlying causes, helping you predict future outcomes and make proactive decisions.

- **Analyze Trends Over Time**: Look for upward or downward trends in time-series data, which indicate growth, decline, or stability.
- **Identify Seasonal Patterns**: In certain industries, data may show seasonal patterns, such as higher sales during holidays or peaks in website traffic at certain times of day.
- **Compare Categories**: For categorical data, compare groups to see if there are any recurring patterns among them, such as higher performance in a specific region or among certain demographics.

Example

If customer complaints spike every December, this pattern could suggest seasonal service issues. Recognizing this allows management to investigate and potentially allocate additional resources during peak times.

Step 4: Interpret Relationships and Correlations

Relationships between variables, such as correlations, can provide deeper insights into cause and effect, revealing factors that might influence performance, behavior, or outcomes.

- **Correlations**: A positive or negative correlation between two variables, such as advertising spend and sales, can indicate potential causal relationships.
- **Comparative Analysis**: Examining relationships between groups (e.g., demographics or regions) helps uncover factors contributing to differences in outcomes.
- **Causal Links**: While correlation doesn't equal causation, understanding potential causal links helps generate hypotheses that can be tested further.

Example

If data shows a strong correlation between customer satisfaction
and issue resolution time, it may indicate that faster response times
contribute to higher satisfaction, suggesting that improving
response efficiency could enhance customer experience.

Common Pitfalls in Data Interpretation

Misinterpreting data can lead to misguided decisions and incorrect
conclusions. Recognizing common pitfalls ensures your
interpretation remains accurate and reliable.

1. Confusing Correlation with Causation

Just because two variables move together doesn't mean one causes
the other. While correlations can suggest potential relationships,
further investigation is needed to establish causation.

2. Ignoring Context

Data points don't exist in isolation—they're part of a broader
context. Ignoring external factors, such as economic changes or
seasonal effects, can lead to oversimplified conclusions.

3. Overlooking Outliers

Outliers can sometimes reveal important insights. Ignoring them
may cause you to miss unusual but significant patterns. However,
outliers should be carefully examined to determine if they're
meaningful or simply errors.

Example

A company might observe a spike in sales in a particular month and assume it's due to a marketing campaign, overlooking the fact that the spike coincided with a major holiday season. Failing to account for this context could lead to misattributing success to the wrong factor.

Telling the Story Behind the Data

Once patterns, trends, and relationships have been identified, the next step is to communicate the insights clearly and effectively. Storytelling with data is about connecting numbers to real-world outcomes, translating data into a narrative that resonates with stakeholders.

Elements of Effective Data Storytelling

1. **Start with the Big Picture**: Begin by summarizing the main insight or message. This helps set the stage for deeper analysis and clarifies the focus of your story.
2. **Provide Context**: Explain the data's background and relevance. Describe the data source, the period covered, and any external factors influencing the numbers.
3. **Highlight Key Insights**: Point out significant findings, such as trends, patterns, or correlations. Emphasize insights that answer the original business question and support decision-making.
4. **Draw Conclusions and Recommendations**: Conclude with specific takeaways and, if possible, actionable recommendations. Tying insights to concrete actions gives the story purpose and helps move stakeholders toward informed decisions.

Example

A company analyzing customer churn might tell the following story: "Over the past year, customer churn rates have increased, especially among younger customers. Analysis shows that these customers are less engaged with the loyalty program. We recommend enhancing the loyalty program to appeal more to younger demographics, which could improve retention."

This storytelling approach not only highlights the main finding (higher churn among younger customers) but also provides context, insight, and an actionable recommendation.

Using Data for Decision-Making

After interpreting the data and telling its story, the final step is using these insights to make informed decisions. Data-driven decision-making ensures that actions are based on evidence rather than assumptions.

Steps for Data-Driven Decision-Making

1. **Evaluate the Insights**: Assess the validity and significance of the insights. Consider whether additional data or further analysis is needed to confirm the findings.
2. **Assess Options and Scenarios**: Based on the data, evaluate possible options or strategies. Consider how each scenario aligns with business goals and constraints.
3. **Implement Decisions and Monitor Outcomes**: Once a decision is made, track its impact and adjust as necessary. Monitoring results ensures that actions are effective and allows for quick responses to unforeseen changes.
4. **Review and Reflect**: Regularly review data to evaluate the ongoing effectiveness of decisions. Reflection supports

continuous improvement and allows for proactive adjustments.

Example

An e-commerce company observes a trend of high cart abandonment rates on mobile devices. After reviewing the data, the team decides to optimize the mobile checkout process. Post-implementation monitoring shows a 15% reduction in abandonment rates, validating the decision to improve the mobile experience.

Case Study: Data-Driven Decision-Making in Action

Imagine a healthcare provider wants to improve patient satisfaction. The team collects data from patient feedback surveys and identifies key factors affecting satisfaction, such as wait times, staff interactions, and facility cleanliness.

Interpreting the Data

1. **Identify Trends**: Survey responses reveal that satisfaction rates are generally lower during peak hours.
2. **Analyze Correlations**: Data shows a strong negative correlation between wait times and satisfaction scores.
3. **Recognize Patterns**: Patterns indicate that staff interaction quality has the highest impact on satisfaction among all factors.

Making the Decision

Based on the data, the provider decides to:

- Increase staffing during peak hours to reduce wait times.
- Implement staff training programs focused on enhancing patient interaction.

Monitoring the Impact

After implementing these changes, the provider tracks satisfaction scores. Within three months, scores improve by 20%, confirming that the data-driven decision was effective in enhancing patient satisfaction.

Key Takeaways

Interpreting data effectively requires moving beyond raw numbers to uncover the underlying story. By understanding patterns, relationships, and trends within data, decision-makers can make informed, evidence-based choices. The key elements of successful data interpretation and decision-making include:

- **Defining the Goal**: Start with a clear question or purpose to guide your interpretation.
- **Identifying Patterns and Trends**: Look for recurring behaviors and changes over time to understand underlying dynamics.
- **Recognizing Relationships**: Correlations and comparisons reveal important connections between variables.
- **Communicating Insights**: Use data storytelling to convey findings in a clear, engaging way.
- **Making Informed Decisions**: Apply insights to drive actions that align with business goals.

Interpreting the story behind the numbers ensures that data is not just a series of values but a valuable resource for understanding the past, managing the present, and planning for the future. With strong data interpretation skills, you can transform complex data into actionable insights that make a real impact.

Avoiding Common Pitfalls in Data Interpretation

Data interpretation is a critical step in deriving insights, but even skilled analysts can fall into common traps that distort findings and lead to misleading conclusions. Avoiding these pitfalls ensures that insights are accurate, that patterns and trends are correctly identified, and that decisions are based on solid evidence rather than misconceptions or errors. In this section, we'll examine some of the most common pitfalls in data interpretation and provide strategies for avoiding them.

1. Confusing Correlation with Causation

One of the most common pitfalls in data interpretation is assuming that correlation implies causation. Just because two variables appear to move together doesn't mean one causes the other. Correlation simply indicates a relationship, not that one variable is responsible for changes in the other.

Example

Suppose a company notices that ice cream sales and sunscreen purchases increase at the same time every year. While these variables are correlated, buying sunscreen doesn't cause ice cream sales to rise. Both trends are driven by a third factor: warmer weather.

How to Avoid This Pitfall

- **Look for Other Influencing Factors**: Consider external or underlying factors that may be influencing both variables.
- **Use Causal Analysis Techniques**: To establish causation, use experimental or causal analysis methods, such as A/B testing, where you control for variables to isolate effects.
- **Avoid Overinterpretation**: When reporting correlated variables, clearly indicate that correlation does not imply causation unless further evidence supports it.

2. Ignoring Outliers

Outliers are data points that deviate significantly from other observations. While some analysts remove outliers to simplify their analysis, ignoring them entirely can lead to a loss of important insights. Outliers can sometimes reveal unique cases, errors, or extreme events that are worth investigating.

Example

A delivery service company finds an outlier in delivery times—one order took significantly longer than average. On investigation, they discover it was due to an unexpected weather delay. Ignoring this outlier would miss the insight that extreme weather events can significantly impact delivery performance.

How to Avoid This Pitfall

- **Investigate Outliers**: Always investigate outliers to understand whether they are data entry errors, natural variations, or indicative of underlying issues.
- **Document Decisions**: If you decide to remove outliers, document the rationale and ensure that it is consistent across analyses.

- **Use Robust Measures**: Use statistical measures that are less sensitive to outliers, such as the median or interquartile range, to supplement mean and standard deviation.

3. Overgeneralizing Findings

Overgeneralizing occurs when conclusions from a specific dataset or population are applied too broadly. This pitfall can lead to inaccurate conclusions if the sample is not representative or if the findings are interpreted as universally applicable without sufficient evidence.

Example

A survey conducted among college students shows a preference for digital textbooks. Overgeneralizing this finding to all age groups could lead to incorrect assumptions about general textbook preferences, as older populations may have different preferences.

How to Avoid This Pitfall

- **Understand Sample Limitations**: Consider the demographics and characteristics of your sample and recognize any limitations in how representative it is of the broader population.
- **Use Multiple Data Sources**: Whenever possible, cross-validate findings with data from other sources to ensure broader applicability.
- **Clearly Define Scope**: Clearly state the scope of your findings and avoid making broad claims unless they are supported by additional evidence.

4. Cherry-Picking Data

Cherry-picking involves selectively using data points that support a particular conclusion while ignoring data that doesn't. This can lead to biased interpretations and distort findings, often resulting in confirmation bias—where you see only what you expect or want to see.

Example

A company analyzing sales growth focuses only on months with high sales to demonstrate consistent growth, ignoring months with lower sales. This cherry-picking creates an incomplete picture and could mislead stakeholders about actual performance trends.

How to Avoid This Pitfall

- **Examine All Relevant Data**: Avoid filtering data in ways that exclude relevant information. Include both supporting and contradicting data in your analysis.
- **Use Transparent Analysis Methods**: Make your methodology transparent so that others can see which data points were included and excluded.
- **Challenge Your Assumptions**: Actively seek out data that challenges your assumptions to reduce the likelihood of confirmation bias.

5. Misinterpreting Averages

Averages, such as the mean, provide a useful summary but can be misleading if not interpreted carefully. Averages can hide important variations or create a skewed impression if there are significant outliers or if data is distributed unevenly.

Example

An employer looks at the average salary in a department and assumes all employees earn around this amount. However, high salaries among senior managers may raise the average, masking lower salaries among entry-level employees.

How to Avoid This Pitfall

- **Use Multiple Measures of Central Tendency**: Consider using the median or mode along with the mean to get a more accurate picture, especially if the data is skewed.
- **Examine the Distribution**: Look at data distribution to see if there are significant deviations from the average or clusters around certain values.
- **Consider Variability**: Use measures like standard deviation or range to understand the spread of data around the average.

6. Failing to Provide Context

Numbers and statistics rarely speak for themselves; without context, they can easily be misinterpreted. Context includes factors like the time period, geographic scope, industry trends, and external influences that may affect data.

Example

A sudden increase in website traffic may seem positive at first glance. However, without the context that this increase was due to a temporary marketing campaign, stakeholders might overestimate the long-term trend.

How to Avoid This Pitfall

- **Provide Background Information**: Explain the context of the data, including any relevant events, timeframes, or market conditions.
- **Use Annotations**: In visuals, add annotations to explain notable data points, like campaign launches or policy changes, that may impact interpretation.
- **Compare to Benchmarks**: Compare data to industry benchmarks or historical trends to give stakeholders a more realistic view.

7. Misleading with Data Visualizations

Visualizations can enhance understanding, but poor design choices can also mislead viewers. Common pitfalls in data visualization include manipulating axis scales, using overly complex charts, or choosing inappropriate colors, all of which can distort interpretation.

Example

A bar chart with a truncated y-axis exaggerates differences between values, making changes seem more dramatic than they are. This can lead to incorrect assumptions about the significance of those changes.

How to Avoid This Pitfall

- **Use Consistent Scales**: Start axes at zero whenever possible, especially for bar charts, to avoid exaggerating differences.
- **Choose the Right Visualization**: Select chart types that accurately represent the data, such as using line charts for trends over time and bar charts for category comparisons.

- **Simplify and Avoid Clutter**: Avoid overly complex visuals and focus on clarity. Use colors and labels sparingly to avoid overwhelming viewers.

8. Ignoring Small Sample Sizes

When interpreting data, it's essential to consider sample size. Small sample sizes can lead to unreliable results and increase the risk of drawing incorrect conclusions due to random variations.

Example

A company tests a new feature with a sample of only 10 users and concludes that it's popular based on a high approval rate. With such a small sample, the results are unlikely to represent the larger customer base accurately.

How to Avoid This Pitfall

- **Use Larger Samples When Possible**: Ensure your sample size is adequate to draw statistically significant conclusions. Larger samples reduce the likelihood of random error.
- **Acknowledge Limitations**: If you must work with a small sample, acknowledge this limitation in your interpretation and be cautious about generalizing findings.
- **Consider Statistical Confidence**: Use statistical tests to measure confidence levels and margins of error, especially in decision-making.

9. Neglecting Time-Series Analysis for Temporal Data

For data that changes over time, such as sales figures or website traffic, failing to consider time-series trends can result in missing key patterns. Without time-based analysis, it's easy to overlook seasonality or trends that affect long-term performance.

Example

An analyst looks at monthly sales figures without recognizing that sales tend to peak every December due to holiday shopping. Without time-series analysis, this seasonal trend goes unnoticed, and forecasts may underestimate expected sales.

How to Avoid This Pitfall

- **Analyze Trends Over Time**: Use time-series analysis methods to identify trends, seasonality, and cyclical patterns in data.
- **Compare Year-Over-Year**: When relevant, compare data to the same period in previous years to identify consistent seasonal patterns.
- **Use Moving Averages**: Moving averages help smooth out short-term fluctuations and reveal long-term trends.

10. Making Assumptions Based on Initial Impressions

Data interpretation can be influenced by first impressions or assumptions, leading analysts to overlook deeper insights or alternative explanations. It's easy to fall into this trap, especially when findings seem to confirm pre-existing beliefs or expectations.

Example

A company sees a drop in customer satisfaction and immediately attributes it to recent policy changes. However, a deeper analysis reveals that the decline was driven by seasonal factors unrelated to the policy change.

How to Avoid This Pitfall

- **Take a Comprehensive View**: Look beyond initial impressions and explore multiple potential explanations for observed trends or patterns.
- **Challenge Initial Assumptions**: Test hypotheses with additional data and consider alternative explanations to avoid confirmation bias.
- **Collaborate with Others**: Involve other team members or stakeholders to get diverse perspectives and reduce the risk of one-sided interpretation.

Key Takeaways

Avoiding pitfalls in data interpretation ensures accuracy, reliability, and objectivity in decision-making. Key strategies include:

- **Recognizing Correlation vs. Causation**: Avoid assuming that relationships between variables imply causation.
- **Providing Context and Clarity**: Interpret data with a clear understanding of its context and limitations.
- **Ensuring Data Representativeness**: Consider sample size, distribution, and relevance when generalizing findings.
- **Using Visuals Responsibly**: Design visualizations that enhance understanding without distorting insights.
- **Looking Beyond First Impressions**: Keep an open mind and seek diverse perspectives to validate interpretations.

By being mindful of these pitfalls, analysts and decision-makers can interpret data more accurately, leading to insights that genuinely reflect reality and support informed decisions.

Applying Data Insights to Real-Life Decision-Making

Data insights are only as valuable as the actions they inspire. In today's data-driven world, businesses, governments, and individuals rely on data to inform decisions, predict trends, and solve problems. However, translating insights from raw data into real-life decisions requires a structured approach, thoughtful interpretation, and a keen understanding of context. In this chapter, we'll explore how to effectively apply data insights to real-life decision-making, moving from numbers to actionable strategies.

Why Applying Data Insights Matters

The ultimate purpose of data analysis is to enable informed decision-making. Insights alone are not enough; they must be actionable, relevant, and applied effectively to make a real impact. Applying data insights helps organizations:

1. **Reduce Uncertainty**: Data-driven insights provide concrete evidence that can replace guesswork, enabling decision-makers to proceed with confidence.
2. **Improve Efficiency**: By identifying areas for improvement or optimization, data insights can streamline processes, reduce costs, and increase productivity.
3. **Identify Opportunities and Risks**: Insights reveal trends and potential risks, allowing proactive responses to market shifts, emerging threats, or new growth areas.

4. **Drive Strategic Goals**: Effective data-driven decision-making ensures that daily operations align with long-term strategic goals.

Let's dive into how to turn insights into action and apply them in various real-life scenarios.

Key Steps for Applying Data Insights to Decisions

Applying data insights to decision-making involves a structured process that ensures insights are both relevant and actionable.

Step 1: Define the Objective

Start by defining the objective. Clear objectives ensure that data interpretation aligns with the organization's needs, guiding the analysis toward actionable insights. Consider what you're trying to achieve, the problem you're solving, or the decision that needs to be made.

Example

An e-commerce company wants to improve its customer retention rate. Defining the objective as "increasing customer retention by 10% in the next quarter" provides a specific goal that guides analysis.

Step 2: Gather Relevant Data

Collect the data most relevant to your objective. This could involve customer data, market trends, historical performance, or survey results. Using data that directly relates to your goal ensures that insights are actionable.

Example

For the customer retention goal, relevant data might include purchase frequency, product satisfaction ratings, customer support interactions, and loyalty program participation. These data points can reveal what influences retention.

Step 3: Identify Key Insights and Patterns

Once the data is prepared, analyze it to identify key insights. Look for trends, correlations, and patterns that can inform your decision. Use visualization tools like bar charts, line charts, and scatter plots to make patterns more apparent.

Example

The analysis shows that customers who engage with the company's loyalty program are 20% more likely to make repeat purchases. Additionally, customers who have positive experiences with customer support are more likely to remain loyal.

Step 4: Develop Actionable Recommendations

Based on the insights, create specific, actionable recommendations that address the objective. Recommendations should be clear, practical, and directly linked to the data insights.

Example

To increase retention, the company could:

1. **Enhance the Loyalty Program**: Offer more rewards and personalized incentives to encourage repeat purchases.
2. **Improve Customer Support**: Implement training to improve customer support interactions and introduce follow-up messages after support cases are resolved.

Step 5: Implement Decisions and Monitor Outcomes

Put the recommended actions into practice. Implementation should include clear timelines, responsibilities, and measurable milestones. Once actions are in place, monitor outcomes closely to measure success and make adjustments as needed.

Example

The company launches an improved loyalty program and sets a quarterly review process to track retention rates. Weekly check-ins on customer support metrics help ensure that improvements are having the intended effect on customer satisfaction.

Real-Life Applications of Data-Driven Decision-Making

Let's explore practical examples of how different industries apply data insights to real-life decisions.

1. Retail: Optimizing Inventory Management

Retail businesses rely heavily on data to manage inventory levels, predict demand, and reduce waste. Data-driven inventory management uses sales trends, seasonality, and customer preferences to make stocking decisions.

Example

A clothing retailer analyzes historical sales data to identify peak demand seasons for specific products, such as winter coats in the colder months. The retailer uses this data to optimize inventory orders, reducing overstocking and preventing stockouts. As a result, the store minimizes storage costs and increases sales by ensuring products are available when customers want them.

Key Insights

- **Seasonality**: Winter coats peak in sales from November through February.
- **Customer Preferences**: Certain styles and colors sell faster, suggesting high demand and guiding stocking decisions.

Decision

Based on these insights, the retailer adjusts inventory orders to stock more winter coats in November, reducing excess inventory during warmer months and boosting profit margins.

2. Healthcare: Improving Patient Care

In healthcare, data analysis helps providers identify patient needs, track outcomes, and improve treatment protocols. Healthcare data insights can reveal trends in patient visits, common health conditions, and areas for service improvement.

Example

A hospital uses data from patient surveys and electronic health records to identify factors influencing patient satisfaction. The data shows that wait times for appointments significantly impact patient satisfaction. By addressing this, the hospital reduces patient churn and enhances care quality.

Key Insights

- **Wait Time Impact**: Long wait times are correlated with lower patient satisfaction scores.
- **Patient Preferences**: Patients prefer earlier appointment slots, suggesting potential adjustments in scheduling.

Decision

The hospital decides to hire additional staff during peak hours and implement a scheduling system that prioritizes shorter wait times, resulting in higher patient satisfaction and improved retention.

3. Marketing: Increasing Campaign Effectiveness

Marketing teams use data insights to optimize campaigns, target the right audiences, and maximize return on investment (ROI). Analysis of metrics like click-through rates, conversion rates, and engagement can reveal which strategies are most effective.

Example

A marketing team analyzes past campaigns and finds that social media ads targeting specific age groups yield higher engagement and conversions than general ads. They also discover that video ads are 40% more effective than static images.

Key Insights

- **Audience Segmentation**: Ads targeting younger demographics have a higher conversion rate.
- **Content Type**: Video ads outperform static ads, suggesting a preference for dynamic content.

Decision

Based on these insights, the team allocates more budget to social media ads targeting younger demographics and produces more video content. This data-driven adjustment results in higher engagement and conversion rates, optimizing marketing ROI.

4. Manufacturing: Enhancing Production Efficiency

In manufacturing, data insights help optimize production processes, reduce downtime, and improve quality. Analyzing data from sensors, production logs, and maintenance records can reveal bottlenecks and inefficiencies.

Example

A manufacturing company analyzes production line data and finds that one machine frequently malfunctions, leading to production delays. By identifying patterns in downtime and repair records, the company decides to replace the aging machine, improving overall efficiency.

Key Insights

- **Frequent Downtime**: The machine has more frequent breakdowns during peak production periods.

- **Repair Costs**: Maintenance costs for this machine exceed those of other machines, making it a candidate for replacement.

Decision

The company invests in a new machine and establishes a preventive maintenance schedule, reducing downtime and boosting production efficiency.

5. Human Resources: Improving Employee Retention

HR departments use data to monitor employee satisfaction, track turnover, and identify retention strategies. Analyzing engagement survey results, performance data, and turnover trends helps HR teams address issues that impact employee morale.

Example

An HR team reviews engagement survey data and exit interview feedback, finding that employees in specific departments feel undervalued due to a lack of growth opportunities. The data suggests that offering development programs could improve retention in these departments.

Key Insights

- **Growth Opportunities**: Employees cite career advancement as a key factor in job satisfaction.
- **Departmental Differences**: Certain departments have higher turnover rates, suggesting targeted interventions.

Decision

The HR team implements a development program for employees in high-turnover departments, including training workshops and clear paths for advancement. Retention rates improve as employees feel more invested in their roles.

Best Practices for Applying Data Insights in Real Life

To effectively apply data insights in decision-making, consider these best practices:

1. **Ensure Data Quality**: Accurate data is the foundation of reliable insights. Verify data quality by checking for accuracy, consistency, and completeness.
2. **Communicate Insights Clearly**: Use visuals, summaries, and clear language to present insights in an accessible way. Effective communication ensures that stakeholders understand the findings and can act on them.
3. **Involve Stakeholders in Interpretation**: Engage stakeholders early to ensure insights are relevant and actionable. Involving team members from different departments also brings diverse perspectives that enhance decision-making.
4. **Consider Long-Term Implications**: When applying insights, think about long-term impacts as well as short-term gains. This approach ensures that decisions align with strategic goals and sustainability.
5. **Be Open to Iteration**: Data-driven decisions should be revisited as new data becomes available. Be prepared to adapt strategies as circumstances change and new insights emerge.

Key Takeaways

Applying data insights effectively requires thoughtful planning, clear objectives, and a structured approach. By moving from insight to action, organizations can make data-driven decisions that:

- **Align with Goals**: Ensure decisions support broader strategic objectives, from customer retention to operational efficiency.
- **Address Real Needs**: Use data to solve specific problems or seize opportunities, creating value and addressing pressing needs.
- **Drive Continuous Improvement**: Data-driven decision-making is iterative, allowing teams to adjust strategies based on ongoing analysis.

When applied thoughtfully, data insights become powerful tools for real-life decision-making, transforming raw data into practical solutions that drive success. By following these steps and best practices, you'll be able to leverage data to make informed decisions that have a lasting impact.

Chapter 8: Hands-On Analytics: Sample Projects

Project 1: Analyzing a Simple Dataset with Excel

Excel is one of the most widely used tools for data analysis due to its accessibility, flexibility, and powerful set of functions. For beginners, Excel provides an excellent introduction to hands-on analytics, enabling users to manipulate data, create visualizations, and draw insights from simple datasets. In this project, we'll work with a sample sales dataset to demonstrate fundamental analytical techniques. By the end of this exercise, you'll be comfortable using basic Excel functions, creating charts, and interpreting key insights.

Project Overview

In this project, we'll analyze a sample dataset containing sales information for an imaginary retail company. The dataset includes details such as product category, sales amount, region, and date. Our goal is to explore the dataset, perform calculations to summarize sales performance, and create visualizations to uncover trends and insights.

Project Objectives:

1. Summarize and interpret key metrics, such as total sales and sales by category.
2. Identify top-performing products and regions.
3. Visualize trends over time using charts.
4. Present findings in a clear, organized format.

Step 1: Importing and Exploring the Dataset

1.1 Import the Dataset

To begin, open Excel and import the dataset. If the data is in a .csv file:

1. Go to **File** > **Open** and select the .csv file to load it in Excel.
2. Alternatively, go to **Data** > **Get External Data** > **From Text/CSV** and select the file.

Once imported, your dataset should appear in a table format, with headers such as **Date**, **Region**, **Product Category**, **Product Name**, **Units Sold**, and **Sales Amount**.

1.2 Explore the Dataset

Start by taking a moment to review the dataset and understand its structure. Familiarize yourself with the columns:

- **Date**: The transaction date.
- **Region**: The geographical location where the sale occurred.
- **Product Category**: Type of product sold (e.g., Electronics, Clothing, Home Goods).
- **Product Name**: Name of the product.
- **Units Sold**: Quantity of the product sold.
- **Sales Amount**: Total revenue from the sale.

Exploring the dataset helps you identify any inconsistencies or data issues, such as missing values, that need to be addressed.

Step 2: Cleaning and Preparing the Data

Before analyzing the data, ensure it's clean and formatted correctly.

2.1 Check for Duplicates

- Go to **Data** > **Remove Duplicates** and select all columns to ensure that there are no duplicate entries. This step prevents overcounting sales.

2.2 Handle Missing Values

- Look for any blank cells, especially in key columns like **Sales Amount** or **Units Sold**. If there are any, fill in missing values with "0" or use Excel's **Filter** tool to filter out incomplete rows.

2.3 Format Data Correctly

- Ensure that **Date** is in the correct date format, and **Sales Amount** is formatted as currency. Highlight the column, right-click, select **Format Cells**, and choose **Currency** or **Date**.

With a clean and formatted dataset, you're ready to start analyzing.

Step 3: Calculating Key Metrics

Excel provides several functions to quickly calculate metrics like total sales, average sales, and sales by category.

3.1 Calculate Total Sales

- In a new cell, use the **SUM** function to calculate total sales:

```excel
Copy code
```

```
=SUM(F2:F1000)
```

This formula calculates the total revenue across all sales records.

3.2 Calculate Average Sales per Transaction

- In another cell, use the **AVERAGE** function to calculate the average sales amount:

```
excel
Copy code
=AVERAGE(F2:F1000)
```

This gives an idea of the average transaction value.

3.3 Summarize Sales by Product Category

- To see total sales by category, use a **PivotTable**:
  - Select your data range.
  - Go to **Insert > PivotTable** and select a new worksheet.
  - Drag **Product Category** to the **Rows** area and **Sales Amount** to the **Values** area.
  - Set the **Values** field to show the **Sum** of Sales Amount.

The PivotTable summarizes sales by each category, showing which categories generate the most revenue.

3.4 Find the Top-Performing Product

- Within the same PivotTable, add **Product Name** under **Product Category** to see sales totals for each product.

- Sort the **Sales Amount** column in descending order to easily identify the top-performing product in each category.

These calculations provide a snapshot of the company's sales performance, identifying which categories and products drive the most revenue.

Step 4: Visualizing Data Insights

Charts help communicate insights visually, making it easier to spot trends and patterns.

4.1 Create a Bar Chart for Sales by Category

- Select the **Product Category** and **Sales Amount** columns from your PivotTable.
- Go to **Insert > Chart** and select **Bar Chart**.
- Customize the chart title to "Sales by Product Category" and add data labels if needed.

This bar chart shows the sales contribution of each product category, making it easy to compare performance.

4.2 Create a Line Chart to Show Sales Trends Over Time

- To analyze monthly sales trends, first create a **PivotTable** with **Date** in the **Rows** area and **Sales Amount** in the **Values** area.
- Adjust the **Date** field settings to group data by **Months**.
- With the PivotTable results, go to **Insert > Line Chart** and select a simple line chart.
- Customize the chart title to "Monthly Sales Trends."

This line chart reveals seasonal trends, growth patterns, and any potential sales peaks or dips over the year.

4.3 Create a Pie Chart for Sales by Region

- In your PivotTable, drag **Region** to the **Rows** area and **Sales Amount** to the **Values** area to summarize sales by region.
- Select the region data and go to **Insert > Chart > Pie Chart** to create a pie chart.
- Label the chart as "Sales by Region" and add data labels to show the percentage of total sales for each region.

The pie chart provides a visual breakdown of sales distribution by region, helping identify top-performing regions.

Step 5: Interpreting the Results

Now that you've calculated key metrics and created visualizations, it's time to interpret the results. Consider the following questions as you analyze the charts and tables:

1. **Which Product Category Performs Best?**
   - From the bar chart, identify the category with the highest sales. For example, if Electronics leads, this may indicate high customer demand, and the company might consider expanding the electronics product line.
2. **What are the Sales Trends Over Time?**
   - Examine the line chart to see if there are any seasonal patterns. If sales peak during certain months, such as December, the company could

increase inventory or offer promotions in anticipation of high demand.

3. **Which Regions Drive the Most Sales?**
   - o The pie chart shows sales distribution by region. If one region generates a disproportionately high amount of sales, the company might focus marketing efforts or inventory adjustments there to maximize revenue.

4. **Which Products Contribute Most to Revenue?**
   - o In the PivotTable, sort products by sales to find the top sellers. These popular items could be included in promotions or bundled with other products to boost revenue.

Step 6: Presenting Your Findings

To present the findings clearly and concisely, create a summary report with the following sections:

1. **Executive Summary**: Briefly outline the main findings, such as the best-performing product category, overall sales trends, and top regions.
2. **Key Metrics**: Summarize total sales, average sales, and other key figures in a small table or as bullet points.
3. **Visualizations**: Include the bar chart, line chart, and pie chart in your report with descriptive titles.
4. **Recommendations**: Based on the insights, suggest actionable steps. For example:
   - o Increase inventory in high-demand months.
   - o Focus marketing efforts in top regions.
   - o Expand the electronics category due to its high sales.

Example Summary Report

Executive Summary: "Sales for the year totaled $500,000, with Electronics as the top-performing category. Sales peak in December, likely due to holiday demand, and Region A contributes 40% of overall sales. To capitalize on these trends, we recommend expanding inventory during peak months and increasing marketing focus in Region A."

Key Takeaways

This project demonstrates how to analyze a simple dataset using basic Excel functions and tools. By calculating key metrics, creating visualizations, and interpreting insights, you can gain a comprehensive view of performance and make data-driven decisions. Key takeaways include:

- **Basic Calculations**: Use functions like SUM and AVERAGE to derive key metrics quickly.
- **PivotTables**: Summarize data and gain insights with ease.
- **Charts and Visuals**: Create bar charts, line charts, and pie charts to visualize insights.
- **Interpreting Results**: Translate findings into actionable recommendations that guide decision-making.

This hands-on project provides foundational skills for analyzing datasets in Excel, setting you up for more advanced analytics projects in the future.

Project 2: Creating a Visualization with a Free Tool (Google Data Studio)

Google Data Studio is a free, web-based tool that enables users to create interactive and visually appealing reports and dashboards. With its integration capabilities and customizable features, Google Data Studio is ideal for visualizing data in ways that are easy to understand and share with others. In this project, we'll walk through the steps to create a simple dashboard in Google Data Studio, using a sample dataset to showcase fundamental visualization techniques.

Project Overview

In this project, we'll use a sample dataset of website analytics for a fictional e-commerce company. The dataset includes metrics such as website traffic, user engagement, and conversions, which we'll use to create charts, tables, and a summary dashboard. By the end of this project, you'll have a solid understanding of how to use Google Data Studio's features to create effective data visualizations.

Project Objectives:

1. Connect a dataset to Google Data Studio and understand its interface.
2. Create visualizations such as line charts, bar charts, and scorecards.
3. Design an interactive dashboard that presents website analytics.
4. Interpret insights from the visualizations to make data-driven decisions.

Step 1: Setting Up Google Data Studio

1.1 Sign Up for Google Data Studio

To get started, you'll need a Google account. Visit Google Data Studio and sign in with your Google credentials. Google Data Studio is free, and using it requires no downloads as it operates entirely in the cloud.

1.2 Familiarize Yourself with the Interface

The Google Data Studio interface includes the following key areas:

- **Data Sources**: Where you connect to various data sources, such as Google Analytics, Google Sheets, or CSV files.
- **Report Canvas**: The main area where you design your report and place charts and visuals.
- **Toolbar**: Tools for adding elements like charts, scorecards, and images to your report.
- **Properties Panel**: Allows you to adjust settings, including chart types, data fields, and formatting options.

Step 2: Connecting Your Dataset

Google Data Studio can connect to multiple data sources. For this project, we'll use a Google Sheet containing our sample e-commerce analytics data, including fields like **Date**, **Sessions**, **Page Views**, **Conversions**, and **Revenue**.

2.1 Set Up Your Data Source

1. Open Google Sheets and create a new sheet with your sample data, or import a .csv file into Google Sheets. Be sure your data has a header row.
2. In Google Data Studio, click on **Create > Data Source**.
3. Select **Google Sheets** and choose your data file from Google Drive.
4. Confirm your data source settings, ensuring that each field (like Date, Sessions, Revenue) is recognized correctly. Adjust field types if necessary (e.g., make sure dates are recognized as **Date** and numeric fields as **Number** or **Currency**).

2.2 Connect Your Data Source to the Report

Once your data source is set up, click **Connect**. Your data is now available for use in creating visualizations on the report canvas.

Step 3: Creating Basic Visualizations

With your data connected, you can now add charts and visuals to your dashboard. We'll start by creating a few key visualizations, including a line chart for website traffic trends, a scorecard to display total revenue, and a bar chart for conversion rates by region.

3.1 Add a Scorecard for Total Revenue

Scorecards are a simple yet powerful way to display key metrics at a glance.

1. Go to the report canvas and click **Add a chart > Scorecard**.

2. Position the scorecard on the canvas where you want it to appear.
3. In the **Data** panel, select **Revenue** as the metric to display.
4. Customize the scorecard to display currency formatting in the **Style** tab.
5. Label the scorecard as "Total Revenue."

This scorecard provides an instant snapshot of total revenue, a key metric for any e-commerce business.

3.2 Create a Line Chart for Website Traffic Trends

A line chart is ideal for visualizing website sessions over time.

1. Click **Add a chart > Time series** and place it on the canvas.
2. In the **Data** panel, select **Date** as the **Dimension** and **Sessions** as the **Metric**.
3. Customize the date range in the **Date Range** section if needed (e.g., to show the last six months).
4. Use the **Style** tab to adjust colors, line thickness, and add data points for emphasis.

This line chart displays traffic trends, helping identify high-traffic periods and seasonal fluctuations.

3.3 Add a Bar Chart for Conversions by Region

Bar charts are useful for comparing categorical data, such as conversions by region.

1. Click **Add a chart > Bar chart** and place it on the canvas.

2. In the **Data** panel, select **Region** as the **Dimension** and **Conversions** as the **Metric**.
3. Adjust sorting options to show the highest converting regions at the top.
4. Use the **Style** tab to adjust the bar colors and add data labels for clarity.

This bar chart shows which regions drive the most conversions, highlighting where the business may focus additional marketing efforts.

3.4 Add a Pie Chart for Device Breakdown

A pie chart can show the distribution of sessions across different devices (e.g., mobile, desktop, tablet).

1. Click **Add a chart > Pie chart** and position it on the canvas.
2. Select **Device Type** as the **Dimension** and **Sessions** as the **Metric**.
3. Customize the chart's color scheme and add data labels to display percentages.

This pie chart reveals the proportion of sessions by device, indicating whether the website is more popular on mobile or desktop, which can inform responsive design decisions.

Step 4: Customizing the Dashboard Layout

Now that you have your key metrics and visualizations, it's time to arrange and style the dashboard to make it visually appealing and easy to interpret.

4.1 Arrange Charts Logically

Place scorecards at the top for quick reference, followed by charts in a logical order. For instance, start with traffic trends, then conversions by region, and finally device breakdown. This layout guides the viewer through the data in a logical flow.

4.2 Add Filters for Interactivity

Adding filters allows users to customize the view, such as by adjusting the date range or filtering by region.

1. Click **Add a control > Date range control** to add a date filter. Position it near the top of the dashboard so viewers can easily adjust the reporting period.
2. To add a region filter, click **Add a control > Filter control** and set **Region** as the dimension.
3. Position the filter controls at the top of the dashboard for easy access.

These interactive controls allow users to explore the data by different time periods or focus on specific regions.

4.3 Apply Styling for Visual Consistency

Use the **Style** tab to apply consistent colors, fonts, and borders. A clean, consistent design improves readability and ensures that the dashboard looks professional.

- **Color Scheme**: Choose a color scheme that aligns with the company's branding. For example, use a different color for each chart type (e.g., green for revenue, blue for sessions).

- **Text and Labels**: Use concise titles and descriptions for each chart. Labels should be clear and informative, such as "Monthly Sessions" or "Top Converting Regions."

Step 5: Interpreting Insights from the Dashboard

With your dashboard complete, you can now analyze and interpret the data insights provided by each visualization.

Insights and Analysis

1. **Website Traffic Trends**: The line chart may show a steady increase in sessions with a peak in certain months, such as during a holiday season or a recent marketing campaign.
2. **Total Revenue**: The scorecard provides an at-a-glance view of total revenue, helping assess overall performance.
3. **Conversions by Region**: The bar chart reveals which regions are converting at higher rates, suggesting areas for targeted marketing efforts or localized content.
4. **Device Breakdown**: The pie chart indicates which devices are most popular among users. If mobile sessions are high, investing in mobile optimization could improve user experience and conversions.

Example Summary

"Our analysis reveals that website traffic peaks during December, likely due to seasonal promotions, and Region A leads in conversions. Mobile users account for 60% of sessions, suggesting that further investment in mobile optimization could increase conversions."

Step 6: Sharing the Dashboard

One of the strengths of Google Data Studio is the ease with which you can share dashboards with others.

1. Click **Share** in the top-right corner of the report.
2. Choose to share via email or create a shareable link. You can set permissions to control who can view or edit the report.
3. For regular updates, set up automated data refresh options so the dashboard stays up-to-date without requiring manual updates.

Sharing the dashboard allows team members to access real-time insights and make data-driven decisions collaboratively.

Key Takeaways

This project demonstrates the basics of using Google Data Studio for data visualization. Key takeaways include:

- **Connecting Data**: Link data from various sources, including Google Sheets, to create a dynamic dashboard.
- **Creating Visuals**: Use different chart types—scorecards, line charts, bar charts, and pie charts—to present a comprehensive view of data.
- **Interactive Filters**: Add filters to enhance interactivity, allowing users to customize the data view.
- **Insights and Actions**: Translate data into actionable insights that inform decisions, such as focusing on high-converting regions or optimizing for mobile users.

Google Data Studio's flexibility and ease of use make it an ideal tool for beginners and professionals alike. By completing this project, you'll be able to create insightful dashboards that visualize data effectively, making it accessible and actionable for decision-makers.

Guidance on How to Present Findings

Data analysis is valuable only when its insights are clearly and effectively communicated. Presenting findings involves more than displaying charts and graphs; it requires a structured approach that connects data-driven insights to specific objectives and actions. Whether you're presenting to stakeholders, team members, or clients, your goal is to ensure that your findings are understandable, relevant, and actionable. In this section, we'll explore best practices for structuring presentations, storytelling with data, and tailoring communication to your audience.

1. Know Your Audience

The first step in presenting findings is understanding your audience's needs, preferences, and technical familiarity with the data. Different audiences require different levels of detail, technicality, and focus. Knowing who you're speaking to enables you to customize the presentation to their level of understanding, ensuring your insights are relevant and clear.

Key Audience Considerations

- **Technical Expertise**: For a technical audience, include details on data sources, methodology, and analysis techniques. For a non-technical audience, focus more on key insights, actions, and results rather than technical specifics.
- **Goals and Interests**: Identify the goals of your audience. For example, an executive team may want insights into

revenue growth, while a marketing team may be more interested in customer engagement metrics.

- **Decision-Making Authority**: Tailor recommendations to the decision-making power of your audience. If they can implement changes directly, your presentation can include tactical actions. If they are senior leaders, focus on strategic insights and broad implications.

2. Structure Your Presentation for Clarity

A well-structured presentation guides your audience through your analysis in a logical sequence, from background to insights to recommended actions. This approach keeps the audience engaged and helps them understand the progression from data collection to insights.

Suggested Presentation Outline

1. **Introduction**: Begin with the objective of the analysis. Briefly explain what you set out to understand or solve, providing context for the audience.
2. **Methodology and Data Overview** (optional): For a technical audience, provide an overview of your data sources, sample size, and methodology. Keep this section concise for non-technical audiences.
3. **Key Findings**: Present the main insights, supported by visuals and data points. Focus on findings that directly relate to your objectives.
4. **Analysis and Interpretation**: Explain what the findings mean and why they matter. Avoid jargon and simplify complex concepts.

5. **Recommendations**: Based on your findings, suggest specific, actionable steps. Recommendations should align with the goals and capabilities of your audience.
6. **Conclusion**: Summarize key takeaways and reinforce the next steps or actions the audience should consider.

3. Tell a Story with Your Data

Storytelling is an effective way to communicate data insights, making them more memorable and impactful. A good data story provides context, meaning, and relevance, helping your audience understand the "why" behind the numbers.

Elements of a Strong Data Story

- **Context**: Begin with background information that sets the stage, explaining why the analysis was conducted and what problem or question you aimed to address.
- **Insight**: Highlight key findings in a way that builds interest. Use charts and visual aids to show how data supports each insight, moving from simple observations to deeper analysis.
- **Impact**: Describe the implications of the insights. For instance, "An increase in website traffic during holiday promotions led to a 20% increase in conversions," linking data to business outcomes.
- **Next Steps**: Conclude with recommendations that flow naturally from your findings, guiding the audience on what to do next based on the insights.

Example of a Data Story

"Last quarter, we noticed a sharp increase in website traffic, particularly during our holiday sales campaign. Analyzing the data further, we found that the majority of this traffic came from mobile devices. However, mobile conversions were lower than desktop conversions, suggesting a potential friction in the mobile experience. By improving mobile site speed and optimizing the checkout process, we can likely boost mobile conversions and increase revenue during peak sales periods."

This narrative connects findings to practical recommendations and anticipated outcomes, making the data more relatable and actionable.

4. Use Visuals Effectively

Visuals are powerful tools for communicating data insights, but they must be carefully designed to avoid confusion or misinterpretation. Choosing the right chart type, simplifying visual elements, and using consistent formatting all contribute to clarity and impact.

Best Practices for Effective Visuals

- **Choose the Right Chart**: Use line charts for trends over time, bar charts for category comparisons, pie charts for proportions, and scatter plots for correlations. Selecting the right chart helps your audience understand the data more quickly.
- **Focus on Key Data Points**: Highlight important data points or trends with bold colors or annotations. This approach directs attention to the most significant insights.
- **Limit Colors**: Stick to a consistent color scheme, using bright colors only to highlight specific data points. Avoid

using too many colors, as this can distract from the main message.
- **Label Clearly**: Ensure that each chart has a clear title, axis labels, and data labels where needed. Labels provide context and prevent misinterpretation.

Example

A line chart showing monthly revenue over a year can be enhanced by highlighting the holiday season months in a different color. This highlights seasonal revenue peaks, making it easy for the audience to see the impact of holiday promotions.

5. Summarize Key Takeaways

After presenting your findings, summarize the key takeaways in a concise manner. Summaries reinforce the main points, helping the audience remember the most important insights and understand their implications.

Tips for Summarizing Key Takeaways

- **Be Concise**: Focus on the most impactful insights that are directly relevant to the audience's goals.
- **Use Bullet Points**: Bullet points or short phrases can make key takeaways easy to remember and visually accessible.
- **Emphasize Actionable Points**: Highlight any actions or recommendations that the audience should consider following the presentation.

Example Summary

"Key Takeaways:

- Holiday campaigns significantly boost website traffic and revenue, with a 30% increase in December.
- Mobile traffic outpaced desktop but had lower conversion rates, suggesting a need for mobile optimization.
- Focusing on high-converting regions can yield better returns from targeted marketing efforts."

6. Offer Actionable Recommendations

Data insights should lead to action. Providing clear, actionable recommendations based on your findings makes it easier for your audience to move from insight to implementation. Each recommendation should be specific, practical, and directly related to your analysis.

Crafting Effective Recommendations

- **Link to Findings**: Make sure each recommendation ties back to a specific insight from your analysis.
- **Be Specific**: Avoid vague recommendations. Instead of saying "improve marketing efforts," specify "increase ad spend in high-converting regions."
- **Prioritize**: Rank recommendations by importance or feasibility. If the audience has limited resources, focus on the actions with the highest potential impact.

Example Recommendations

Based on findings from a sales performance analysis:

1. **Enhance Mobile Experience**: Improve mobile site speed and streamline the checkout process to increase mobile conversions by an estimated 15%.

2. **Target High-Performing Regions**: Focus marketing efforts on regions with higher conversion rates to maximize ROI.
3. **Plan for Seasonal Demand**: Increase inventory and staffing levels during the holiday season to accommodate higher demand and boost sales.

7. Be Ready for Questions

Your audience may have questions that require clarification or additional detail. Being prepared to answer questions ensures that you can address any uncertainties, provide deeper insights, and reinforce the credibility of your findings.

Tips for Handling Questions

- **Anticipate Common Questions**: Think ahead about what questions may arise based on your analysis. Be prepared to discuss methodology, data sources, or deeper implications.
- **Use Data to Support Answers**: If possible, refer to specific data points or visuals in your presentation to support your answers.
- **Clarify Limitations**: If questions address areas outside the scope of your analysis, clarify any limitations and offer to investigate further if needed.

Example

If a stakeholder asks why mobile conversions are lower than desktop conversions, you might explain, "Our analysis suggests that checkout friction may be a factor, as mobile users experience slower load times. We recommend optimizing mobile site speed to improve the user experience and potentially increase conversions."

8. Follow Up with a Summary Report

After the presentation, provide a summary report that captures the key insights, visuals, and recommendations. A summary report reinforces your presentation's findings and serves as a reference for decision-makers as they consider next steps.

Elements of a Good Summary Report

- **Executive Summary**: A brief overview of the objectives, findings, and recommendations.
- **Key Insights and Visuals**: Include charts and graphs that were part of the presentation to illustrate main points.
- **Recommendations**: Outline actionable steps based on the insights, with any prioritization noted.
- **Contact Information**: Make it easy for readers to follow up with questions by including your contact details.

Example of a Summary Report

An executive summary might read, "This report provides insights into website traffic trends, with a focus on increasing conversions. Key findings include high traffic during the holiday season, lower mobile conversion rates, and strong performance in specific regions. We recommend optimizing the mobile experience and focusing marketing efforts in high-converting areas to drive future growth."

Key Takeaways

Presenting findings is a vital step in data analysis that bridges the gap between insights and action. By structuring your presentation, using effective storytelling, and focusing on actionable recommendations, you can ensure that your analysis is both understood and impactful. Key takeaways include:

- **Understand Your Audience**: Tailor your presentation to the audience's technical level and decision-making needs.
- **Use Storytelling Techniques**: Present data in a way that flows logically and engages your audience.
- **Emphasize Key Findings and Recommendations**: Highlight the most important insights and link them to clear, actionable steps.
- **Be Prepared for Follow-Up**: Address questions confidently and provide a summary report for future reference.

Effective presentation of data findings makes it easier for stakeholders to understand and act on insights, leading to more informed and successful decision-making. By mastering these skills, you'll enhance the value of your data analysis and ensure your insights lead to meaningful results.

Chapter 9: Pathways to Intermediate Data Skills

Databases, Programming, and Advanced Statistics

Once you have a solid foundation in data analysis, the next step is to develop more advanced skills that can help you handle larger datasets, automate processes, and perform sophisticated analyses. Mastering databases, programming, and advanced statistical techniques will enable you to work with complex data, enhance your analytical capabilities, and take on more challenging projects. In this chapter, we'll explore the essential intermediate skills in these areas, providing a pathway to expand your analytical toolkit.

1. Working with Databases

Databases are crucial for managing large datasets efficiently, enabling storage, retrieval, and manipulation of data at scale. As data grows in volume and complexity, understanding database structures and learning how to interact with databases using SQL (Structured Query Language) is essential for any data analyst.

Key Concepts in Databases

- **Relational Databases**: Relational databases store data in structured tables with defined relationships between them, which makes it easy to organize and query information. Examples include MySQL, PostgreSQL, and Microsoft SQL Server.
- **Database Schema**: The schema defines the structure of a database, including tables, fields, and relationships. Understanding schema design is important when working with multiple tables and joining data.

- **SQL**: SQL is the primary language used to interact with relational databases, allowing users to query, update, and manipulate data.

Essential SQL Skills

1. **Basic Queries**: Learn to select, filter, and sort data using commands like SELECT, WHERE, ORDER BY, and LIMIT.
2. **Joins**: Mastering JOIN operations is crucial, as it allows you to combine data from multiple tables. Common types of joins include INNER JOIN, LEFT JOIN, and RIGHT JOIN.
3. **Aggregation Functions**: Functions like SUM, COUNT, AVG, and GROUP BY enable you to calculate totals, averages, and other summary statistics.
4. **Subqueries**: Subqueries are queries within queries, allowing you to perform complex filtering and aggregations.
5. **Data Manipulation**: Learn commands like INSERT, UPDATE, and DELETE to modify data within the database.

Example: Querying Sales Data

Suppose you have a database with tables for **Customers**, **Orders**, and **Products**. You could use SQL to find the total sales by region, the top-selling products, or the most frequent customers.

```sql
SELECT region, SUM(order_total) AS total_sales
FROM Orders
JOIN Customers ON Orders.customer_id = Customers.customer_id
GROUP BY region
ORDER BY total_sales DESC;
```

This query provides a summary of sales by region, helping the company identify its most profitable locations.

Learning Resources

- **Online Courses**: Platforms like Coursera, Udacity, and DataCamp offer SQL courses for beginners to advanced levels.
- **SQL Practice Websites**: Websites like SQLBolt and Mode Analytics provide interactive exercises to reinforce SQL skills.
- **Hands-On Projects**: Practice by setting up a database with sample data and running queries to answer business questions.

2. Introduction to Programming for Data Analysis

Programming adds power and flexibility to data analysis, enabling you to automate tasks, handle large datasets, and perform complex calculations. Python and R are two of the most popular languages for data analysis due to their extensive libraries, versatility, and supportive communities.

Why Learn Programming?

Programming allows you to:

- **Automate Repetitive Tasks**: Write scripts to automate data cleaning, transformations, and repetitive calculations.
- **Process Large Datasets**: Handle data too large for spreadsheet tools like Excel, especially with libraries that optimize data manipulation.

- **Create Custom Visualizations**: Build unique charts and dashboards tailored to specific needs.
- **Perform Advanced Analytics**: Use statistical and machine learning libraries to build predictive models and uncover deeper insights.

Getting Started with Python

Python is a beginner-friendly language with a broad ecosystem of libraries suited to data analysis. Here are some essential Python libraries for data analysts:

1. **Pandas**: Used for data manipulation and analysis. It provides functions for reading, cleaning, filtering, and aggregating data.
2. **NumPy**: Supports numerical calculations and is particularly useful for handling large datasets and performing mathematical operations.
3. **Matplotlib and Seaborn**: These libraries are commonly used for data visualization, enabling you to create line charts, bar charts, histograms, and more.
4. **Scikit-Learn**: A powerful machine learning library for predictive analysis, clustering, and regression.

Example: Analyzing Customer Data with Python

Suppose you have a dataset of customer purchases in a CSV file. You could use Python and Pandas to analyze customer spending patterns.

```python
import pandas as pd

# Load data
data = pd.read_csv("customer_purchases.csv")

# Calculate average spending by customer
average_spending = data.groupby("customer_id")["purchase_amount"].mean()

# Identify high-spending customers
high_spenders = average_spending[average_spending > 100]
```

This script loads the data, calculates average spending per customer, and identifies customers with average spending over $100.

Learning Resources

- **Online Courses**: Websites like DataCamp, Coursera, and Codecademy offer introductory courses in Python and R for data analysis.
- **Documentation and Tutorials**: The official documentation for libraries like Pandas, Matplotlib, and Scikit-Learn is an excellent resource.
- **Practice Projects**: Try projects like analyzing a dataset with Pandas, building a visualization in Matplotlib, or creating a basic predictive model with Scikit-Learn.

3. Advanced Statistics and Data Analysis Techniques

Advanced statistical skills enable you to draw more robust insights from data and apply sophisticated analytical techniques. Proficiency in statistics is essential for building predictive models, conducting experiments, and making data-driven decisions based on probability and uncertainty.

Key Statistical Concepts for Intermediate Analysts

1. **Probability Distributions**: Understanding distributions like normal, binomial, and Poisson helps in interpreting data and calculating probabilities.
2. **Hypothesis Testing**: Hypothesis testing allows you to make inferences about data, such as determining whether observed differences are statistically significant. Key tests include t-tests, chi-square tests, and ANOVA.
3. **Regression Analysis**: Regression models describe relationships between variables. Common techniques include linear regression, logistic regression, and multiple regression.
4. **ANOVA (Analysis of Variance)**: ANOVA helps you compare means across multiple groups, useful for testing if group differences are statistically significant.
5. **Time Series Analysis**: Time series methods, like moving averages and exponential smoothing, are used to analyze data over time, identify trends, and make forecasts.

Example: Using Regression Analysis to Predict Sales

Suppose you want to predict future sales based on historical data, including advertising spend, seasonality, and product category.

1. Collect and clean your data, ensuring all variables are in a usable format.
2. Use linear regression to model the relationship between advertising spend and sales, incorporating other variables as needed.

3. Interpret the regression coefficients to understand the impact of each variable on sales.

In Python, you can use Scikit-Learn to perform linear regression:

```python
from sklearn.linear_model import LinearRegression

# Define predictors and target variable
X = data[["advertising_spend", "seasonality", "product_category"]]
y = data["sales"]

# Fit the model
model = LinearRegression()
model.fit(X, y)

# Predict future sales
predicted_sales = model.predict(X)
```

This analysis provides insights into the factors driving sales and allows you to forecast future sales based on input variables.

Learning Resources

- **Online Courses**: Look for advanced statistics courses on websites like Udacity, Khan Academy, or Coursera.
- **Books**: Titles like *The Art of Statistics* by David Spiegelhalter and *Practical Statistics for Data Scientists* are valuable resources.
- **Statistical Software**: Explore software like R, which is widely used in academia and offers robust statistical packages.

Bringing It All Together: A Sample Project

To illustrate how databases, programming, and statistics can be combined in an analysis project, let's consider a real-life example:

Sample Project: Customer Segmentation Analysis

Objective: To identify and segment customers for targeted marketing.

Steps:

1. **Data Collection**: Gather customer data, including demographics, purchase history, and engagement metrics. Store this data in a relational database (e.g., MySQL).
2. **Data Preparation**: Use SQL to clean and filter the data, removing duplicates and organizing it by key variables.
3. **Data Analysis in Python**: Use Python to analyze customer spending patterns, calculate average order values, and identify high-value customers. Employ clustering techniques, such as K-Means, to segment customers.
4. **Statistical Analysis**: Perform statistical tests to validate that the segments differ significantly in terms of spending, demographics, and engagement.
5. **Report Findings**: Present findings in a dashboard with charts that illustrate each segment's characteristics. Include actionable insights, such as personalized marketing strategies for each customer group.

Key Takeaways

Expanding your skills in databases, programming, and advanced statistics enables you to tackle more complex data challenges, create custom analyses, and draw deeper insights. Key takeaways include:

- **Database Skills with SQL**: Master SQL to efficiently manage and query large datasets stored in databases.
- **Programming Skills with Python or R**: Use programming to automate tasks, manipulate large datasets, and perform advanced analysis.
- **Advanced Statistical Techniques**: Apply statistical methods to validate findings, make predictions, and draw robust conclusions from data.

These intermediate skills will make you a more versatile analyst, capable of handling complex data scenarios and delivering high-impact insights.

Why Ongoing Learning is Essential in Data Analytics

Data analytics is a dynamic field, constantly evolving with new tools, techniques, and trends. Keeping your skills up to date is crucial for staying relevant, enhancing your career prospects, and improving the quality of your analyses. By committing to continuous learning, you'll be well-equipped to adapt to advancements in data science, explore new methodologies, and confidently tackle more complex data challenges.

1. Build a Continuous Learning Plan

A structured learning plan can help you prioritize skills and allocate time for development. Identify the skills you want to enhance and set specific, measurable goals to track your progress.

Steps to Build Your Learning Plan

1. **Identify Key Areas for Growth**: Reflect on your current skill set and consider which areas you'd like to improve.

These might include advanced statistical techniques, programming languages, or specialized tools like Tableau or SQL.

2. **Set Learning Goals**: Create short- and long-term goals. For example, set a goal to learn the basics of machine learning within three months or master SQL in six months.
3. **Allocate Regular Time for Learning**: Designate a consistent time each week for learning. Even an hour or two can make a significant difference over time.
4. **Assess Your Progress**: Periodically review your progress, evaluate your understanding, and update your learning goals as needed.

Example Learning Plan

Goal: Improve Python programming skills.

- **Timeline**: Three months
- **Steps**:
    o Month 1: Complete a Python fundamentals course
    o Month 2: Practice data analysis with Pandas and NumPy
    o Month 3: Complete a mini-project in Python, such as analyzing a dataset or building a simple visualization

A learning plan like this helps you stay focused and see steady progress in your skill development.

2. Take Advantage of Online Courses and Certifications

Online courses and certifications provide structured, comprehensive learning and help validate your skills to potential employers. Many reputable platforms offer high-quality content taught by industry experts.

Recommended Platforms for Data Analytics

- **Coursera**: Courses from top universities like Stanford, Johns Hopkins, and the University of Washington, covering topics from data science fundamentals to advanced machine learning.
- **Udacity**: Specialized nanodegree programs, including Data Analyst, Machine Learning Engineer, and SQL for Data Analysis.
- **DataCamp**: Interactive courses with a focus on Python, R, SQL, and other data science tools. DataCamp's short exercises and projects are ideal for hands-on learning.
- **edX**: Provides data science courses from institutions like MIT and Harvard, often with an option for certification.
- **Khan Academy and freeCodeCamp**: Excellent free resources for learning the basics of statistics, Python programming, and SQL.

How to Choose the Right Course

- **Evaluate the Syllabus**: Ensure the course covers relevant topics aligned with your learning goals.
- **Check Reviews and Ratings**: Look at reviews from past learners to gauge the course quality and effectiveness.
- **Consider Hands-On Projects**: Select courses that offer practical exercises, projects, or capstone tasks, as hands-on learning is essential in data analytics.

Suggested Certifications

- **Google Data Analytics Professional Certificate**: A beginner-friendly certification covering fundamental data analytics skills.
- **IBM Data Science Professional Certificate**: A comprehensive program that includes Python, SQL, and data visualization.
- **Microsoft Certified: Data Analyst Associate**: Ideal for those focusing on Power BI and data visualization.
- **Certified Analytics Professional (CAP)**: A rigorous, industry-recognized credential for experienced analysts.

These certifications can serve as milestones in your learning journey and enhance your professional credibility.

3. Stay Updated on Industry Trends and Tools

Staying current with industry trends, new tools, and emerging techniques is essential as the data field evolves. Following industry leaders, reading relevant content, and joining online communities can keep you informed and inspired.

Sources for Staying Updated

- **Blogs and News Sites**: Sites like KDnuggets, Towards Data Science, Analytics Vidhya, and Data Science Central regularly publish articles on the latest developments in data science.
- **Industry Reports**: Organizations like Gartner, McKinsey, and the International Institute for Analytics publish reports on trends and technologies impacting the data analytics field.

- **Newsletters**: Sign up for newsletters like Data Elixir, O'Reilly Data & AI Newsletter, and Analytics Weekly to receive curated content on data science and AI.
- **YouTube Channels**: Channels like StatQuest with Josh Starmer, Corey Schafer, and Sentdex offer tutorials and explanations on a range of data science topics, including programming, statistics, and machine learning.

Tip: Set Up Google Alerts

Use Google Alerts to get notifications on topics like "data analytics trends," "machine learning tools," or "Python for data science." This will keep you up to date on developments that matter most to your career goals.

4. Join Data Science Communities and Networks

Communities provide a space to exchange ideas, seek help, and connect with other data enthusiasts. Networking within data science communities allows you to learn from others' experiences, gain insights into best practices, and even discover career opportunities.

Recommended Data Science Communities

- **Kaggle**: Kaggle is one of the largest data science communities, offering datasets, competitions, and discussion forums where members share solutions and collaborate.
- **Reddit**: Subreddits like r/datascience, r/statistics, and r/learnpython are active communities where users share resources, ask questions, and discuss industry trends.

- **Stack Overflow**: A valuable resource for troubleshooting coding issues and finding solutions to technical challenges in Python, SQL, and other languages.
- **LinkedIn Groups**: Join LinkedIn groups like Data Science Central, Big Data and Analytics, and Python Developers to stay updated on industry news, participate in discussions, and network with professionals.
- **Meetup.com**: Look for local data science or machine learning groups that host events, webinars, and networking opportunities. Meeting people in person or virtually can be an excellent way to expand your knowledge and connections.

Benefits of Community Engagement

- **Learning from Peers**: See how others approach data problems, and learn from their experiences.
- **Getting Feedback**: Share your work and get constructive feedback, which can help you improve.
- **Access to Resources**: Communities often share helpful resources like articles, tutorials, and code libraries.
- **Job Opportunities**: Networking can open doors to job referrals, freelance gigs, or project collaborations.

5. Practice with Real-World Data Projects

Applying your skills to real-world data projects is one of the best ways to deepen your knowledge. Projects give you hands-on experience, build your portfolio, and demonstrate your capabilities to potential employers.

Types of Projects to Consider

- **Data Cleaning and Transformation**: Work with messy, real-world datasets to practice data cleaning techniques like handling missing values, standardizing formats, and restructuring data.
- **Exploratory Data Analysis (EDA)**: Use a dataset from Kaggle or a public source to explore relationships, trends, and patterns. EDA projects showcase your ability to derive insights from data.
- **Predictive Modeling**: Build simple models using regression, classification, or clustering to predict outcomes or segment data. Predictive projects highlight your understanding of machine learning basics.
- **Data Visualization**: Create a dashboard in Tableau, Power BI, or Google Data Studio to display KPIs for a specific dataset. Visualization projects demonstrate your ability to communicate insights effectively.

Resources for Finding Project Datasets

- **Kaggle**: Offers thousands of datasets on topics from sports to healthcare, ideal for analysis, modeling, and visualization projects.
- **UCI Machine Learning Repository**: Provides free datasets frequently used in machine learning research.
- **Google Dataset Search**: A search engine that helps you find datasets across the web.
- **Government Databases**: Sites like Data.gov (US), Data.gov.uk (UK), and the World Bank provide public datasets on economics, health, environment, and more.

6. Keep a Portfolio of Your Work

Building a portfolio is essential for showcasing your skills to potential employers. A portfolio demonstrates your ability to analyze, visualize, and interpret data and serves as a record of your progress over time.

Elements of a Strong Data Portfolio

- **Project Descriptions**: Provide a brief summary of each project, including objectives, data sources, methods, and key insights.
- **Code and Documentation**: Include code snippets or links to code repositories (e.g., GitHub) to demonstrate your technical skills.
- **Visualizations and Reports**: Share charts, dashboards, or reports that illustrate your ability to communicate data insights effectively.
- **Personal Website or GitHub**: Consider setting up a personal website or a GitHub profile to host your portfolio and make it accessible to recruiters.

Example Project for Portfolio

Project: Customer Segmentation Analysis

- **Objective**: Segment customers based on purchasing behavior to inform targeted marketing.
- **Methodology**: Used K-Means clustering to identify customer groups, performed EDA, and visualized findings in a Tableau dashboard.
- **Outcome**: Identified three main customer segments with distinct spending habits, leading to personalized marketing strategies.

7. Experiment with New Tools and Techniques

The data analytics field is continuously introducing new tools, libraries, and techniques. Experimenting with these innovations can expand your skills and keep you adaptable.

Tools and Techniques to Explore

- **New Programming Libraries**: Try libraries like Plotly for interactive visualizations, PyCaret for automated machine learning, or NLTK for natural language processing.
- **Cloud-Based Analytics**: Platforms like Google BigQuery, Amazon Redshift, and Microsoft Azure offer cloud-based data storage and analytics capabilities.
- **Automated Machine Learning (AutoML)**: Tools like H2O.ai, Google AutoML, and DataRobot simplify the model-building process, allowing you to experiment with predictive modeling without extensive coding.
- **Deep Learning**: If you're ready for advanced concepts, explore TensorFlow or PyTorch to experiment with neural networks and deep learning models.

Key Takeaways

To remain competitive in the data analytics field, continuous learning is essential. By following these strategies, you can stay updated, broaden your skills, and keep pace with industry advancements:

- **Build a Structured Learning Plan**: Set clear goals, dedicate regular time, and review your progress.
- **Leverage Online Resources**: Use courses, certifications, and tutorials to learn at your own pace.

- **Stay Updated with Industry News**: Follow blogs, reports, and newsletters to keep up with trends and developments.
- **Engage with Communities**: Participate in data science forums, meetups, and online groups to learn and network.
- **Practice with Real-World Projects**: Develop practical skills by working on projects and building a portfolio.
- **Experiment with New Tools**: Explore new libraries, platforms, and technologies to expand your capabilities.

By committing to ongoing learning, you'll be prepared to tackle future data challenges, stay ahead of industry trends, and achieve lasting success in your data analytics career.

Why Data Literacy is Essential Across All Careers

Data literacy—the ability to read, work with, interpret, and communicate data—is a valuable skill in virtually every profession today. Whether you're in business, healthcare, education, or marketing, understanding how to use data empowers you to make informed decisions, solve problems efficiently, and contribute to data-driven strategies. In this chapter, we'll explore how data literacy applies to a range of careers, offering specific tips and examples for leveraging data effectively in each field.

1. Data Literacy in Business and Management

In business and management, data literacy enables professionals to make strategic decisions, identify opportunities for growth, and optimize resources. Data-driven decision-making has become a cornerstone of competitive advantage, as it helps leaders understand customer behavior, market trends, and operational efficiency.

Tips for Applying Data Literacy in Business

- **Use Dashboards for Real-Time Monitoring**: Leverage dashboards in tools like Tableau or Power BI to monitor key performance indicators (KPIs) like sales, customer retention, and operational costs. Real-time data allows you to respond quickly to changes and make timely adjustments.
- **Analyze Financial Data for Budgeting and Forecasting**: Use historical financial data to identify spending trends and forecast future budgets. Analyzing expenses by category can help in making cost-cutting decisions without affecting essential operations.
- **Conduct Customer Analysis**: Use data from CRM (Customer Relationship Management) systems to analyze customer behavior, preferences, and purchasing patterns. Insights from customer segmentation can guide marketing strategies and improve customer engagement.

Example

A sales manager might use data from a CRM system to identify high-value customers and focus sales efforts on these segments. Analyzing customer data by region, spending habits, and engagement history can help prioritize leads and tailor sales pitches to different groups.

2. Data Literacy in Healthcare

Healthcare professionals use data to improve patient outcomes, streamline hospital operations, and track treatment effectiveness. Data literacy enables healthcare providers to make evidence-based decisions and respond proactively to patient needs.

Tips for Applying Data Literacy in Healthcare

- **Monitor Patient Outcomes**: Use data on patient recovery rates, readmission statistics, and treatment effectiveness to adjust care protocols and improve outcomes.
- **Optimize Resource Allocation**: Analyze data on hospital occupancy, staffing levels, and equipment usage to optimize resource allocation and reduce wait times.
- **Conduct Predictive Analysis**: Use patient data to predict health outcomes and identify at-risk patients. Predictive modeling can help in early intervention and preventive care planning.

Example

A hospital administrator might use data to track patient wait times in the emergency department. By analyzing peak times and average waiting durations, they can adjust staffing schedules to ensure adequate support during busy periods, improving patient satisfaction and reducing congestion.

3. Data Literacy in Marketing

Marketing professionals rely heavily on data to understand customer behavior, track campaign performance, and optimize advertising strategies. Data literacy allows marketers to make targeted decisions and improve ROI on campaigns by identifying which strategies work best.

Tips for Applying Data Literacy in Marketing

- **Track Campaign Performance Metrics**: Use tools like Google Analytics to track metrics such as click-through

rates, conversions, and customer engagement. Regular analysis helps refine targeting and improve future campaigns.
- **Conduct A/B Testing**: Use data-driven experiments to test different ad creatives, email headlines, or landing page designs. A/B testing allows you to determine which version performs better based on actual user behavior.
- **Segment Audiences for Personalized Campaigns**: Segment your customer base by demographics, purchasing history, or engagement level to create targeted campaigns. Audience segmentation enables marketers to tailor messages and improve relevance.

Example

A digital marketing team might analyze conversion data to find that certain demographics respond better to specific messaging. By segmenting their audience and personalizing content, they can increase engagement and optimize advertising spend for a better return on investment.

4. Data Literacy in Finance and Accounting

In finance, data literacy enables professionals to analyze financial health, detect fraud, and forecast future performance. Data-driven insights are crucial for managing risk, identifying growth opportunities, and ensuring regulatory compliance.

Tips for Applying Data Literacy in Finance

- **Analyze Financial Ratios**: Use financial ratios like profit margin, return on assets, and debt-to-equity ratio to assess company health and make comparisons with industry benchmarks.

- **Implement Risk Analysis Models**: Use statistical analysis to evaluate risk and model potential scenarios. For example, calculating Value at Risk (VaR) helps assess the probability of a financial loss.
- **Forecast with Historical Data**: Use historical data to project future performance, budget requirements, and cash flow. Forecasting enables proactive planning and investment decisions based on reliable trends.

Example

A financial analyst might use trend analysis on historical revenue data to predict next quarter's revenue. By identifying seasonal fluctuations, the analyst can create a more accurate forecast and inform strategic decisions, such as adjusting budget allocations for marketing during peak periods.

5. Data Literacy in Human Resources

HR departments use data to manage workforce performance, improve employee retention, and optimize recruitment strategies. Data literacy empowers HR professionals to make informed, people-centered decisions and improve organizational culture.

Tips for Applying Data Literacy in HR

- **Analyze Employee Turnover**: Use data on employee tenure, exit interviews, and department turnover rates to understand why employees leave and develop retention strategies.

- **Measure Employee Engagement**: Conduct and analyze employee engagement surveys to identify areas for improvement. Engagement data can reveal patterns related to job satisfaction, work-life balance, and organizational culture.
- **Optimize Recruitment Strategies**: Use data on time-to-hire, recruitment sources, and applicant demographics to improve hiring practices and reduce costs associated with employee turnover.

Example

An HR manager might analyze turnover data to find that a specific department has a higher-than-average turnover rate. After identifying potential causes, such as workload or lack of development opportunities, the manager can implement targeted retention strategies, such as training programs or work-life balance initiatives.

6. Data Literacy in Education

In education, data literacy helps educators improve student outcomes, track engagement, and make data-informed decisions about curriculum and teaching methods. Analyzing educational data supports student success and enhances learning experiences.

Tips for Applying Data Literacy in Education

- **Track Student Performance Metrics**: Analyze data on test scores, attendance, and engagement to identify areas where students may need additional support.
- **Conduct Curriculum Analysis**: Use feedback and performance data to evaluate curriculum effectiveness.

Identifying which areas are challenging for students can inform curriculum adjustments.

- **Personalize Learning**: Use data on learning styles and progress to create personalized learning plans for students, improving their engagement and success rates.

Example

A teacher might analyze assessment data to identify topics where students consistently score lower. This data could suggest a need for additional resources, different teaching strategies, or one-on-one tutoring for students struggling with certain concepts.

7. Data Literacy in Supply Chain and Operations

In supply chain and operations, data literacy enables professionals to optimize inventory management, streamline logistics, and reduce costs. By analyzing data on production, transportation, and inventory, companies can improve efficiency and meet customer demands effectively.

Tips for Applying Data Literacy in Supply Chain

- **Monitor Inventory Levels**: Use data to track inventory turnover rates, reorder points, and demand patterns. Data-driven inventory management reduces costs associated with overstocking or stockouts.
- **Optimize Logistics**: Analyze transportation data to identify cost-saving opportunities, such as route optimization, fuel usage, and carrier performance.
- **Forecast Demand**: Use historical sales data to forecast demand accurately. Demand forecasting allows for better production planning and inventory control.

Example

An operations manager might analyze seasonal sales data to identify peak periods and adjust inventory accordingly. By aligning inventory with anticipated demand, the company can avoid stockouts during high-demand periods and minimize excess inventory in off-peak seasons.

8. Data Literacy in Product Development

Product development teams use data to understand customer needs, assess product performance, and guide innovation. Data literacy in this field supports product design, testing, and continuous improvement based on real-world usage patterns and feedback.

Tips for Applying Data Literacy in Product Development

- **Analyze User Feedback**: Collect and analyze customer feedback data to identify common issues and areas for improvement.
- **Conduct Usage Analysis**: Track user behavior data to understand how customers interact with a product, which features are most popular, and which are underutilized.
- **Perform A/B Testing**: Use data-driven experiments to test different product features or designs. A/B testing allows you to assess which options perform best with users.

Example

A product manager might analyze usage data to find that a specific feature is not being used as expected. This insight could lead to redesigning the feature or providing user education to enhance its usability and encourage adoption.

Key Takeaways

Data literacy is a versatile skill that enhances decision-making, problem-solving, and strategy in every field. By leveraging data effectively, professionals can drive improvements, anticipate challenges, and create value for their organizations. Key takeaways include:

- **Business and Management**: Use data to drive strategy, optimize resources, and understand customer behavior.
- **Healthcare**: Apply data to improve patient outcomes, optimize resource allocation, and plan preventive care.
- **Marketing**: Use data insights to refine targeting, personalize campaigns, and track campaign success.
- **Finance**: Conduct risk analysis, assess financial health, and forecast trends using data.
- **Human Resources**: Use data to analyze turnover, measure engagement, and improve recruitment.
- **Education**: Track student performance and personalize learning to improve educational outcomes.
- **Supply Chain and Operations**: Optimize inventory, streamline logistics, and accurately forecast demand.
- **Product Development**: Analyze user feedback and conduct testing to enhance product features and usability.

Data literacy empowers you to unlock insights and make informed decisions, no matter your field. By applying these tips, you'll be able to leverage data more effectively in your career, enhance your professional impact, and contribute to data-driven success in your organization.

Conclusion and Resources

Summary of Key Takeaways

As you reach the end of this journey into data literacy, it's worth reflecting on the key insights and skills you've gained. Mastering data literacy opens doors to new opportunities, enhances your decision-making, and allows you to drive positive changes in your field. Here's a summary of the core takeaways from each section:

1. **Understanding Data Basics**: Learning foundational concepts—such as the differences between data, information, and knowledge—forms the building blocks of data literacy. Knowing how to distinguish between data types (qualitative vs. quantitative, structured vs. unstructured) helps you work more effectively with various datasets.

2. **Data Collection and Cleaning**: Data cleaning is an essential step that ensures data accuracy and reliability. Removing duplicates, handling missing values, and standardizing formats prepares your data for meaningful analysis, making it easier to derive reliable insights.

3. **Data Analysis Techniques**: From calculating averages to visualizing trends, understanding data analysis techniques enables you to interpret data accurately. Exploring patterns, identifying correlations, and analyzing trends are all vital skills that provide actionable insights.

4. **Data Visualization**: Visualizing data through charts and graphs allows you to communicate findings clearly. Selecting the right chart type, organizing information logically, and emphasizing key insights make your data accessible and impactful.

5. **Using Data for Decision-Making**: Applying data insights to real-life scenarios, from business to healthcare, empowers you to make informed decisions. By interpreting data in context and understanding its implications, you can drive better outcomes.
6. **Pathways to Advanced Skills**: Developing skills in databases, programming, and advanced statistics enables you to work with complex datasets, automate processes, and perform sophisticated analyses. Expanding your technical knowledge broadens your data capabilities and prepares you for more advanced challenges.
7. **Staying Updated and Lifelong Learning**: Data literacy is an evolving field, making continuous learning essential. By staying informed about industry trends, joining data communities, and setting learning goals, you ensure that your skills remain current and relevant.
8. **Applying Data Literacy Across Careers**: Data literacy enhances your impact in any field, from business and healthcare to education and marketing. By applying data skills strategically, you can solve real-world problems, optimize performance, and contribute to data-driven decision-making in your career.

By mastering these fundamentals, you've gained a comprehensive toolkit to tackle data challenges confidently. Whether you're analyzing customer behavior, predicting financial trends, or personalizing learning experiences, data literacy equips you with the insights needed to make a meaningful impact.

Resources for Continued Learning

Data literacy is a lifelong journey, and there are numerous resources available to help you continue growing your skills. Here are some recommended resources for expanding your knowledge, keeping up with trends, and practicing hands-on data analysis:

1. **Online Learning Platforms**
   - **Coursera**: Offers courses from top universities on data science, machine learning, data analysis, and more.
   - **Udacity**: Known for its nanodegree programs, which offer comprehensive training in data analysis, machine learning, and artificial intelligence.
   - **DataCamp**: Provides interactive courses focused on Python, R, SQL, and data visualization.
   - **edX**: Partnered with universities and institutions to offer data science courses on a wide range of topics.
2. **Certification Programs**
   - **Google Data Analytics Professional Certificate**: A beginner-friendly program covering data analysis fundamentals.
   - **IBM Data Science Professional Certificate**: An in-depth program that includes Python, SQL, and data visualization.
   - **Microsoft Certified: Data Analyst Associate**: Focused on Power BI and data visualization.
   - **Certified Analytics Professional (CAP)**: A recognized certification for advanced analytics professionals.
3. **Books for Deeper Learning**
   - *Storytelling with Data* by Cole Nussbaumer Knaflic: A guide to effective data visualization and data-driven storytelling.

- *Python for Data Analysis* by Wes McKinney: An essential guide for using Python, Pandas, and NumPy for data analysis.
- *The Art of Statistics* by David Spiegelhalter: A beginner-friendly introduction to statistical concepts and their applications.
- *Data Science for Business* by Foster Provost and Tom Fawcett: A book that explains data science concepts in the context of real-world business applications.

4. **Data Science Communities and Forums**
   - **Kaggle**: A platform that provides datasets, competitions, and a community of data science enthusiasts.
   - **Reddit**: Subreddits like r/datascience, r/learnpython, and r/statistics offer discussions, resources, and support for data professionals.
   - **LinkedIn Groups**: Groups like Data Science Central and Big Data & Analytics foster networking and knowledge sharing.
   - **Stack Overflow**: A valuable resource for troubleshooting coding issues, especially for Python, SQL, and R users.

5. **Practice Datasets and Project Ideas**
   - **Kaggle Datasets**: Thousands of datasets on diverse topics, from healthcare to finance, ideal for practice and projects.
   - **UCI Machine Learning Repository**: A well-known source of datasets for machine learning research and practice.
   - **Google Dataset Search**: A search engine that finds datasets across the web.

- o **Data.gov**: A source of public government datasets on economics, health, environment, and more.
6. **Professional Networking and Learning Events**
   - o **Meetup.com**: Search for local data science meetups and webinars to connect with other data professionals.
   - o **Conferences**: Conferences like Strata Data, Data Science Summit, and KDD (Knowledge Discovery in Data) offer learning and networking opportunities.
   - o **Workshops and Hackathons**: Participate in hackathons, like those hosted by Kaggle and DataHack, to apply your skills to real-world problems and compete with peers.

By engaging with these resources, you'll continue to expand your data skills, stay updated with industry changes, and connect with a network of data professionals who can support your learning journey.

Encouragement and Call to Action

You've taken an important step toward data literacy by working through this book and acquiring the foundational skills necessary to read, interpret, and apply data in meaningful ways. Whether you're using data to make strategic decisions, optimize processes, or simply understand the world better, data literacy has empowered you with a new lens for thinking critically, questioning assumptions, and making evidence-based decisions.

As you move forward, remember that data literacy is a journey—one where there is always more to learn, new tools to explore, and deeper insights to uncover. Embrace a mindset of curiosity and growth. The more you practice and apply your skills, the more confident you will become in using data to solve complex problems and make a positive impact.

Here's how you can continue this journey:

1. **Stay Curious**: Ask questions, seek answers in data, and challenge yourself to go deeper. Curiosity is the driving force behind innovation and discovery.
2. **Practice Regularly**: Data skills are like any other skill— the more you use them, the stronger they become. Seek out opportunities to analyze new datasets, try different tools, and tackle real-world problems.
3. **Share Your Insights**: Communicating your findings with others reinforces your learning and adds value to your work. Share your insights with your team, present your analyses confidently, and be open to feedback.
4. **Network and Collaborate**: Engage with the data community to exchange knowledge, find inspiration, and stay motivated. Collaboration with others will expose you to diverse perspectives and broaden your understanding of data applications.

The demand for data-literate professionals is growing in every industry, and by continuing to build your skills, you'll be well-prepared to thrive in a data-driven world. Your journey in data literacy not only enhances your career but also enables you to make a meaningful impact in your field.

Remember, the possibilities with data are limitless—your journey has just begun. Embrace the power of data literacy, and keep exploring, questioning, and growing. The future belongs to those who can turn data into insights, and now you are equipped to be part of that future.

References

1. **Anderson, C. (2015).** *Creating a Data-Driven Organization: Practical Advice from the Trenches.* O'Reilly Media.
   - This book offers practical strategies for building a data-driven culture within organizations, with real-world advice on implementing data literacy and driving analytics adoption.
2. **Camm, J. D., Cochran, J. J., Fry, M. J., & Ohlmann, J. W. (2020).** *Business Analytics.* Cengage Learning.
   - This comprehensive textbook covers foundational concepts in data analytics, including descriptive, predictive, and prescriptive analytics. It's widely used in business analytics courses and provides examples that are relevant across industries.
3. **Chen, C. C., Hardle, W. K., & Unwin, A. (2007).** *Handbook of Data Visualization.* Springer.
   - This handbook provides a thorough exploration of data visualization techniques and best practices, offering both theoretical and practical insights into visualizing complex datasets effectively.
4. **Few, S. (2012).** *Show Me the Numbers: Designing Tables and Graphs to Enlighten.* Analytics Press.
   - This book focuses on effective data visualization design, helping readers understand how to create clear and impactful visuals to support data interpretation and communication.
5. **Han, J., Pei, J., & Kamber, M. (2011).** *Data Mining: Concepts and Techniques.* Morgan Kaufmann.
   - An in-depth guide to data mining techniques, covering foundational and advanced concepts in extracting meaningful patterns from data. This text

is especially useful for readers interested in the technical aspects of data analysis.

6. **Knaflic, C. N. (2015).** *Storytelling with Data: A Data Visualization Guide for Business Professionals.* Wiley.
   - o Knaflic's book is a highly accessible guide to data visualization and storytelling, providing practical tips for creating visuals that effectively communicate insights to non-technical audiences.

7. **McKinney, W. (2017).** *Python for Data Analysis: Data Wrangling with Pandas, NumPy, and IPython.* O'Reilly Media.
   - o This book by the creator of the Pandas library offers a detailed introduction to data manipulation and analysis in Python, making it ideal for readers interested in using Python for data literacy.

8. **Provost, F., & Fawcett, T. (2013).** *Data Science for Business: What You Need to Know About Data Mining and Data-Analytic Thinking.* O'Reilly Media.
   - o A foundational text that connects data science principles to business applications. It covers data-driven decision-making and is accessible for those new to data science.

9. **Siegel, E. (2013).** *Predictive Analytics: The Power to Predict Who Will Click, Buy, Lie, or Die.* Wiley.
   - o Siegel's book explains predictive analytics in an engaging way, demonstrating the impact of predictive modeling across various industries and offering case studies on real-world applications.

10. **Spiegelhalter, D. (2019).** *The Art of Statistics: How to Learn from Data.* Basic Books.
    - o Spiegelhalter's book is an approachable introduction to statistical thinking, helping readers develop the

foundational skills needed for interpreting data insights accurately.

11. **Tufte, E. R. (2001).** *The Visual Display of Quantitative Information.* Graphics Press.
    - A classic text on data visualization principles, Tufte's book provides guidance on creating clear and impactful data visuals, emphasizing design that enhances understanding without adding unnecessary complexity.
12. **Valli, C. (2021).** *Machine Learning with Python Cookbook: Practical Solutions from Preprocessing to Deep Learning.* O'Reilly Media.
    - This resource provides practical solutions and code snippets for data manipulation, feature engineering, and machine learning in Python, suitable for readers looking to build hands-on skills.
13. **Wickham, H., & Grolemund, G. (2016).** *R for Data Science: Import, Tidy, Transform, Visualize, and Model Data.* O'Reilly Media.
    - This book introduces readers to data science in R, focusing on the "tidyverse" approach to data analysis. It's an essential reference for those interested in data literacy through R programming.
14. **Yau, N. (2013).** *Data Points: Visualization That Means Something.* Wiley.
    - Yau's book explores the storytelling aspect of data visualization, with emphasis on creating visuals that reveal insights in meaningful ways. It covers the technical and creative sides of data storytelling.
15. **Zikmund, W. G., Babin, B. J., Carr, J. C., & Griffin, M. (2012).** *Business Research Methods.* South-Western College Publishing.

- o This textbook covers research methods and data collection techniques, offering insights into both qualitative and quantitative data analysis, which are applicable across fields.
16. **Khan Academy** *(n.d.)*. Statistics and Probability. https://www.khanacademy.org
    - o Khan Academy's free online courses on statistics and probability provide accessible resources for learning foundational concepts in data analysis and statistical reasoning.
17. **DataCamp** *(n.d.)*. Data Science and Data Analysis Courses. https://www.datacamp.com
    - o DataCamp offers interactive courses covering data analysis, programming, and machine learning, with hands-on projects and exercises that reinforce data literacy skills.
18. **Kaggle Datasets and Competitions** *(n.d.)*. https://www.kaggle.com
    - o Kaggle provides a vast library of datasets and hosts data science competitions, making it a valuable platform for practice and learning with real-world data.
19. **Google Data Analytics Professional Certificate** *(2021)*. Coursera. https://www.coursera.org/professional-certificates/google-data-analytics
    - o This program, designed by Google, covers foundational data skills, including data cleaning, analysis, and visualization, making it ideal for those seeking a structured introduction to data literacy.

About the author

Dr. Alex Harper is a data scientist, educator, and industry consultant with over 15 years of experience in data analytics, data-driven decision-making, and business intelligence. With a Ph.D. in Information Systems from the University of California, Berkeley, Dr. Harper has held key roles in technology and finance, where they specialized in turning complex datasets into actionable insights that drive growth and innovation.

Throughout their career, Dr. Harper has been passionate about making data accessible to all, regardless of technical background. They have taught data analytics courses at several universities, mentored aspiring data professionals, and spoken at global conferences on topics ranging from data visualization to predictive modeling. Dr. Harper is known for their ability to demystify data concepts, making them relatable and practical for individuals in diverse fields.

Dr. Harper believes that data literacy is a skill everyone can master, and their latest book, *Data Literacy Essentials: From Basics to Practical Applications*, empowers readers to harness data in meaningful ways, no matter their profession. When not working with data, Dr. Harper enjoys hiking, traveling, and exploring culinary arts.

Disclaimer

The information presented in *Essential Data Analytics Quick-Start Guide to Data Literacy for Beginners* is for educational purposes only. While every effort has been made to ensure the accuracy and completeness of the information contained within this book, the author and publisher make no representations or warranties of any kind and assume no liability for any errors or omissions. The data concepts, techniques, and examples provided are intended as general guides and may not be suitable for all situations or applications.

This book does not constitute professional advice, and readers should seek the guidance of qualified professionals regarding any specific data analysis, business, or legal matters. The author and publisher disclaim any liability, personal or professional, for loss or risk incurred as a consequence, directly or indirectly, of the use or application of any of the contents in this book.

All product names, logos, and brands mentioned in this book are property of their respective owners.

Copyright and Legal Notice

Essential Data Analytics Quick-Start Guide to Data Literacy for Beginners

Copyright © [2024] by Dr. Alex Harper

www.ingramcontent.com/pod-product-compliance
Lightning Source LLC
La Vergne TN
LVHW051227050326
832903LV00028B/2268